sunderland
empire
a centenary history

T0351186

sunderland
empire
a centenary
history

Alistair Robinson

First published in 2007 by Tempus Publishing

Reprinted in 2008, 2019 by
The History Press
97 St George's Place, Cheltenham,
Gloucestershire, GL50 3QB
www.thehistorypress.co.uk

British Library Cataloguing in Publication Data.
A catalogue record for this book is available from the British Library.

ISBN 978 0 7524 4340 9

Typesetting and origination by
Tempus Publishing Limited.
Printed in Great Britain by TJ International Ltd, Padstow, Cornwall.

Contents

Introduction

My first memories of Sunderland Empire are happy and vertiginous. Happy, because I was watching Derek Dene in the 1965 *Puss in Boots* panto and he seemed to my seven-year-old mind to be the funniest man alive; and I was close enough for him to reach me with a Quality Street toffee penny. Vertiginous, because every now and then I'd put my head back and look up to the apex of the ceiling and have to steady myself on the arm rests of my seat in the stalls, as I imagined myself falling from that dizzying height.

Twenty-two years later, I sat above that ceiling and looked down through the grill where the chandelier was attached. It was the Empire's eightieth birthday in 1987 and I had been taken on a celebratory ascent of the fly tower by the theatre's technical director, Mel James. The vertiginous thrill was of course heightened; meanwhile, my sense of attachment to the theatre had deepened partly because I was once again clinging on for dear life. By this time though I also had a bond with the Empire through my role as Entertainments Editor for the *Sunderland Echo*. I got to go to the theatre every week, and while I can't say I enjoyed every show as much as I had that *Puss in Boots* panto, I certainly wished every one to succeed. If I was occasionally a stern critic it was only because I felt the Empire and its audience deserved the very best.

During the 1990s however, it became painfully apparent that despite many a fine production, and no matter how many facelifts the Empire received, the theatre seemed always to be on the decline; its great days were in the distant past, its future uncertain. Now that decline has been arrested. A sense of vertigo is induced when we consider the heights to which the theatre has risen in recent years.

The first edition of this book came out as the Empire was making the switch to private management which was to secure its future. This edition has been published to mark the Empire's centenary and to celebrate the remarkable upturn in the theatre's fortunes. In staging this production many people have helped behind the scenes.

George McCarthy and Alan Yardley have been extraordinarily generous and supportive. George supplemented my research by lending me his list of every act to have appeared at the Empire. Alan allowed me to draw on his vast collection of music hall photographs and memorabilia. I am also deeply grateful to Albert Anderson who helped kick-start the first edition of the book, the late Dick Thompson who gave me access to the Thornton family archive, Phil Trusler, Ron Lawson of the Sunderland Antiquarian Society, Harry Packard, Kenneth 'Checker Wheel' Wheal, Odette Stuckey and Derek Walker for supplying prized photographs, Paul Ryan, Mel James, Joanne Wilkins, Stuart Anderson, Chris Alexander, Julie Elliott and Jane Hall from Sunderland Empire and Sunderland City Council, my journalist colleagues Carol Roberton, John Taylor, Julie Barnfather and the *Sunderland Echo* photographic department, particularly Kevin Brady and Susan Swinney, ex-Empire dresser Tom Kershaw, broadcaster Frank Wappat, veteran entertainer Alf Pearson, Laurel and Hardy and Chaplin expert A.J. Marriot, Ella Retford descendant Rebecca Teague, Bobby Thompson's son, Keith, Father John Caden, the late Marjorie Arnfield MBE for access to Milburn family archives, and the late Eva Milburn.

I would like to dedicate this new edition of the book once more to my daughters, Jasmine and Rosanna, but also to my new wife Laura who had to spend the first few weeks of her marriage with me and Wee Georgie Wood.

1

Setting the Scene

Sunderland Empire is Sunderland's gateway to the stars. It's where the world of work and home, the world of bill-paying and house-cleaning, of bus-catching and job-hunting meets the world of celebrity. It's where a Bob or a Vera can walk in off a rainy street on a workaday evening and see, within the Empire's wedding-cake auditorium, with its tiers of seating decorated with mouldings that look like sugar icing, such mythical creatures as Marlene Dietrich, The Beatles or Laurel & Hardy – breathing and gleaming in their own unsung home town. And yet the Empire's stage has also had a democratising effect.

Famously hard to impress, Sunderland folk have been able to bring the stars down to earth: that stage belongs to them, not the famous faces from the telly or silver screen. It has put them on an almost equal footing – a sardonic quip from the wag in the gallery going some way towards bridging the gulf between celebrity and anonymity across the footlights.

Sunderland Empire today is one of a kind. It is Sunderland's only professional theatre. It is the North East's last surviving big-time 'palace of varieties'. It is the largest theatre between Manchester and Edinburgh. Its nearest competitors used to be within a couple of hundred yards of it; they too were big theatres that attracted the biggest stars. Now they are all demolished, as are the sister Empires in Newcastle, Gateshead and Hartlepool. At times Sunderland Empire's isolation has been somewhat desperate. Today it is of the splendid variety as the largest West End shows – *Miss Saigon, Starlight Express, Chitty Chitty Bang Bang* – come to it alone.

Its survival is rightly celebrated. In 1906, as the Empire's foundation stone was being laid, the ground was shifting in the world of entertainment. It was in that year that Sunderland's first cinema, the Monkwearmouth Picture Hall, was opened. It was also in 1906 that the world's first radio programme was broadcast from Brant Rock, Massachusetts. Its highlights might only have been the multi-talented inventor Reginald Fessenden playing *O Holy Night* on his violin and reading a passage from the Bible, but he was merely demonstrating the potential of the medium; others would soon dream up rather more diverting programmes of wireless entertainment that would in coming decades offer a cheap and convenient alternative to a night in the theatre. The development of radio would also of course prepare the ground for television technology. Meanwhile, phonograph cylinders and discs were allowing those who could afford them the chance to hear music in the home, and in 1908, when the Empire had been open only a year the recording industry took another leap forward with the production of the double-sided record disc. Even within the theatre, styles of entertainment were changing. The 'revue', a collection of songs, sketches and dances, often with a topical or satirical slant (the forerunner of today's television sketch shows) was on its way from France to challenge or in some cases supplant the variety bill.

As we shall see, Sunderland Empire was able to survive the coming revolution largely because it was the biggest and most advanced of the theatres and variety halls, but it was not to have an easy life and had to constantly adapt to change.

Opposite above: An audience excitedly awaits curtain-up at Sunderland Empire.

Opposite below: Sunderland's High Street in Edwardian times.

Right: Vesta Tilley with her husband Walter de Frece.

The palaces of varieties had themselves been the big new trend of the late Victorian and early Edwardian period. Their future seemed secure. When the Empire's founders met at the corner of Garden Place and High Street West, Sunderland, on 29 September 1906, with trowel, foundation stone and celebrity guest, it was not with a wary eye on the technological advances of the coming century but in a spirit of utmost confidence.

Sunderland in 1906 was on the rise. One of the country's great industrial towns, home to some of the nation's most famous and productive shipyards, Sunderland had begun to consolidate in the former Bishopwearmouth township, the present city centre. The Empire was one of many grand buildings, including law courts, police station, fire station and offices, that sprang up between 1906 and 1907. It was also one of seven big venues – the others were the People's Palace, Avenue Theatre, King's Theatre, Olympia, Victoria Hall and Theatre Royal – within a few blocks of each other. The King's Theatre was completed just months before the Empire opened. However, changes in entertainment were not the only threat to those venues; strikes and industrial depression were in fact just around the corner.

At the Empire's foundation ceremony, the mayor, aldermen, councillors, leading professionals and captains of industry could feel proud that they were about to build the biggest theatre in the region – the jewel in the crown of local theatre owner Richard Thornton – and had managed to attract comedienne Vesta Tilley, one of the greats of music hall, to be their guest of honour. The doyenne of male impersonators, Tilley was forty-two years of age in 1906 and had been on the stage for thirty-eight of those years, conquering America and the British Empire as well as the Empire theatres. Her husband, leading impresario Walter de Frece, was with her that Saturday in Sunderland.

The Empire's founder – Richard Thornton.

Also among the guests were William and T.R. Milburn, the Sunderland architectural partnership that went on to design many British theatres, including the Dominion in Tottenham Court Road in London. William Milburn told the gathering that their Empire would be 'absolutely up-to-date and behind nothing, either in the provinces or in London'.

The Empire was the pinnacle of Thornton's career. Born in South Shields in 1839, he had begun his working life at the age of ten, sharpening picks alongside his pitman father at St Hilda's Colliery in the town. On weekends he would play the violin at pubs and on the pleasure boats of the Tyne. His first taste of theatre had been in a makeshift auditorium in the cellar of the Locomotive pub in his hometown where boys would pay a penny to watch rather grotesque entertainments, one of which involved a dead cat, enacted against the backdrop of a dusty white sheet. His entry into rather more conventional theatre came when he was engaged as a violinist at the Theatre Royal on King Street, South Shields. Thornton became the leader of the orchestra then moved into pub management and ownership, establishing a music room at the Shakespeare in Union Alley to the rear of the Royal. It was in the Alley in 1885 that he opened his first theatre, Thornton's Varieties, which flourished until 1898 when it made way for his Empire Palace of Varieties.

The Empire's architects, T.R. (left) and William Milburn.

Thornton's own empire had expanded ten years earlier when he had acquired an interest in Sunderland's Theatre Royal from Edward Moss. An alliance was struck between the two men and the Moss Empires company formed. It would become the largest theatre organisation in the world. In 1889-90 they built Newcastle Empire then opened Empires in Birmingham, Sheffield, Liverpool, Glasgow, Hull, Nottingham, Leeds and Bradford. In 1899 as the partnership moved into London and another great theatre owner, Oswald Stoll, added his venues to the chain, Thornton quit to concentrate on his North East Circuit which remained allied to Moss Empires.

After laying the Sunderland Empire foundation stone, Vesta Tilley inspected the plans, signed autographs and was driven away in her car to Newcastle. She would be back on 1 July 1907 for the theatre's opening night.

2

The Curtain Rises

Unlike most theatres, which have auditoriums that present a grand exterior, Sunderland Empire is largely hidden. Built on the former site of the rectory for Bishopwearmouth parish church (now Sunderland Minster) its auditorium is set one block back from High Street West and is bounded by side streets and a back lane. As originally conceived, its only frontage on High Street was its circle and stalls entrance, but it was quite an entrance. Connected to the auditorium by its grand staircase and circular waiting rooms, its front door is in the wall of a 90ft domed tower – said to be inspired by Wren and Hawksmoor – crowned with a 7ft-high statue of the sprightly Terpsichore, the Greek muse of dance, prancing on a revolving steel globe which bore in its early days an illuminated Empire sign. The word Empire was also spelled out in gilded letters on the tower. Two swan-necked electric globe lights cast their glow on to the theatregoers as they entered the building. The Empire proclaimed its presence to the rest of the town.

If it had not been for quick thinking by workmen, however, Sunderland's fancy new theatre might not have survived to welcome its first audience. On the afternoon of Friday 28 June 1907, three days before the opening night, a barrel of tar caught fire on the Empire roof. The fire brigade was called out, but before it arrived the builders had the presence of mind to push the barrel over the edge. It fell to the street and a man who happened to be walking there was splashed by tar but the Empire was saved.

Built at a cost of £31,000, it was not only the biggest theatre in town it was also intended to be the safest, notwithstanding the hazard of flying, flaming tar. Its Sunderland-born architects would have needed no reminding that twenty-four years earlier almost 200 children had died at a show at the Victoria Hall. Rushing to the stage to receive free toys, they had been halted by a bolted door and were either crushed or suffocated in the stampede. The Empire was designed to handle two shows each night and its passageways were so arranged that people entering for the second house would not clash with those leaving the first. Tip-up seats were fitted in the stalls and circle. In the pit and balcony the seats were static but had been carefully arranged to avoid overcrowding. There were electric lights in the auditorium, in the front-of-house, on the stage and in the dressing rooms. There were large, electrically-lit signs over every exit.

The grand main entrance was for those who could afford the more expensive seats; others reached the theatre's pit (now the rear stalls) and the upper circle and gallery by entrances at the rear of the building. Only seats in the posh parts of the theatre could be reserved, so there was usually a rush for the best vantage points of the pit, upper circle and gallery.

As the wealthier customers made their rather more stately progress they encountered a confection of marble and alabaster, Corinthian pilasters and fancy cornice work. The interior of the tower was decorated with painted panels of famous dramatists and musicians. The auditorium was no less ornate, with baroque mouldings everywhere and further painted panels, and the columns and balustrade theme was continued in a domed ceiling and in large, highly ornate boxes, either side of the proscenium arch, that looked like oriental palaces

Above: The corner of Garden Place and High Street West, Sunderland, in about 1901, with a vacant plot that will accommodate the Empire's tower and main entrance, and Bishopwearmouth rectory that will be demolished to make way for the theatre's auditorium. (Picture courtesy of Ron Lawson, Sunderland Antiquarian Society)

Right: The newly built Sunderland Empire.

Left: The Empire's grand staircase and entrance hall in 1907.

Below: The scene that greeted the Empire's first patrons as they entered the circle waiting rooms in 1907.

The Empire stage and interior in pristine condition in 1907

and presented almost as much a spectacle as the on-stage entertainment. The boxes allowed the 'well-to-do' to be seen by the less fortunate in other parts of the house but not to see much of the stage. Beneath them, and also suffering from a restricted view, were the 'slips', or 'slippers', as they became known in Sunderland, where the dress circle swept to the sides of the stage, a distinctive arrangement that had its disadvantages for those brave enough to step into the spotlight.

The Empire seated 3,000 people, 1,000 more than today, and the first performance's capacity crowd was able to fully appreciate this splendour when at 7.15 p.m., just before the show began, the house lights were switched on. The audience was so dazzled that it broke into applause. As this subsided the orchestra struck up the national anthem. The curtain rose and Sunderland entertainer Lilian Lea was centre stage ready to sing *God Save the King*. Behind her, in an august semicircle, were Richard Thornton, Sir Edward Moss and Oswald Stoll, the Milburn brothers and J. W. White, the Empire's builder.

The first act was W. Fullbrook and Co. in *Astronomy,* described on the bill as 'a really farcical sketch scintillating with fun'. Next up was child comedienne Maudie Francis, followed by comedy duo Thorpe and Coe, comedian Charlie Kay, the 'Cyclonic' Sousloff dancers, and Will Van Allen, a resourceful American who tapped out tunes on a dining table.

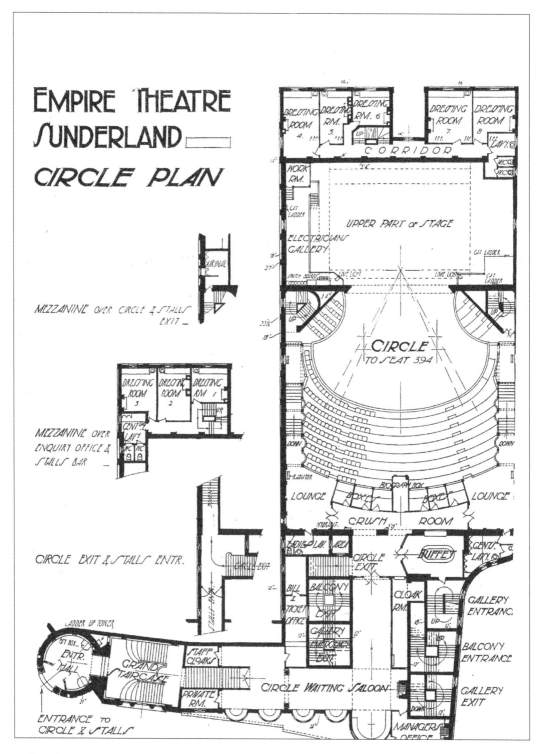

A plan of the Empire published in the 1908 edition of *The Builder* magazine.

The opening night bill.

Vesta Tilley in her many guises.

Vesta Tilley – feminine despite male dress.

But the heartiest reception was reserved for Vesta Tilley, who since her last visit to the town had completed her fourth triumphant tour of America. She came out as 'Piccadilly Johnny' in frock coat and top hat, then became the scarlet-coated soldier 'Tommy Atkins' which had the theatre ringing with applause and laughter, and an 'Eton Schoolboy' which also 'excited tremendous enthusiasm', said the following day's *Sunderland Daily Echo*. Tilley was called back several times, then Richard Thornton stepped on stage to hand her a bouquet of flowers. She also received a bouquet from the children of the architects – nine-year-old Eva, the daughter of T.R. Milburn, the Empire's principal designer, and Vyvien, the son of William Milburn. Ninety years later, Eva, by then, living in a nursing home in Leyburn, North Yorkshire, recalled Vesta as 'a smart little thing'. She added, 'I have a memory of Vesta Tilley saying to my mother, "I would have kissed them both, but I had such heavy makeup on".'

Still the applause rang out for the star of the show. The audience would not let her leave. At last she threw off her coat and said she would 'have another go'. She came back on as 'The Seaside Sultan', an office boy 'on the swank'. Her act, though, was not the final entertainment. The biograph box was proudly unveiled and a moving picture was projected showing her laying the Empire's foundation stone. Lilian Lea then had the unenviable job of following the great star, and her songs and sketches were also 'loudly applauded'. The *Echo* was impressed that at the end of the show the many exits were cleared in a few minutes and the theatre refilled for the second performance. At the second full house Vesta Tilley also received many curtain calls and finally made a speech, thanking the audience.

The *Echo* reviewer concluded that, 'Altogether the new Empire entered on its career under circumstances most auspicious'.

3

The Stars Come Out

The variety hall building boom which spawned Sunderland Empire was the culmination of a half century's progress – although some regretted the passing of the bad old days – during which music hall had moved out of the back rooms of pubs and largely shrugged off its attendant trades of boozing and debauchery.

Richard Thornton and his associates, who had themselves graduated from staging entertainment in the back rooms of pubs, were pioneers in the refinement of music hall, even to the extent of avoiding the very term. Frank Allen, who began as a Monkwearmouth postmaster and ended as one of the most powerful figures in British theatre, boasted, with some justification, that the opening of Thornton's Varieties in South Shields in 1885 was 'a red-letter day in the annals of high-class entertainment'.

Allen, the venue's first manager, explained, 'It witnessed the birth of the family amusement venue. The words "music-hall" we determined to dispense with, substituting "variety theatre" as the hallmark of our scheme. That there might be no mistake regarding the quality of our programmes we topped all our bills with the foreword, "A good, clean entertainment guaranteed here. Bring your wife and family, and enjoy elegance, safety, comfort, and respectability".' This principle was extended to every theatre that Thornton opened and to the entire Moss Empires circuit which Allen ran after Sir Edward Moss's death.

In the Edwardian palaces of varieties future competition in the form of the gramophone and the cinema was at first merely more variety for the bill. As we have seen, the Empire had film shows from the beginning and it soon introduced gramophone background music to the foyer and auditorium. As for the future stars of the silver screen, it was in the provincial palaces that they trained for their Hollywood careers.

W.C. Fields, in the days when he was billed as an 'eccentric juggler', visited Sunderland Empire twice. His first appearance was at the top of a bill in October 1908. He returned in July 1913 with the *Sunderland Daily Echo* remarking on his 'deftness' with balls as well as his sparing skilful use of words that was to be a hallmark of his film career.

Sunderland played a crucial role in Stan Laurel's development as an entertainer. It was at the King's Theatre on Crowtree Road that after a few faltering appearances as a solo comedian in Glasgow he made his stage debut in a touring production. Under his real name of Stanley Jefferson, he was in the cast of *The Sleeping Beauty* which began a national tour at the King's Theatre on 30 September 1907. He played the exalted role of 'Second Golliwog'.

Stan's father, Arthur Jefferson senior, was a theatre manager who had begun as a comedian. By 1907 he was running theatres in North Shields, Blyth, Wallsend, Hebburn and Glasgow but continued to work on stage. With Stan, who had grown up in Bishop Auckland and North Shields, he wrote a comedy sketch called *Home From the Honeymoon*, a story of two tramps who enter a house while the owner is away on holiday. It went out on tour in May 1908 and reached Sunderland Empire on 10 August 1908. Stan does not get a mention in the *Sunderland Daily Echo*

W.C. Fields – eccentric juggler.

review of the show but according to Laurel and Hardy expert A.J. Marriot, it is believed he joined the tour when it was at Newcastle Empire, the week before its trip to Sunderland.

When Charlie Chaplin arrived at Sunderland Empire on 13 April 1908 he was on his third visit to the town. On 22 February 1904 had begun a week at the Avenue Theatre in *Sherlock Holmes*, a play written by the actor William Gillette (who had originated the lead role) and the great sleuth's creator Sir Arthur Conan Doyle. Another actor-writer, H.A. Saintsbury, played Holmes while the fourteen-year-old Chaplin played Billy, the page.

On 15 October 1906 while the builders were busy at the Empire, Chaplin was across the road at the People's Palace, opening in *Casey's Circus* in which a group of versatile young entertainers played urchins, putting on a circus. Sunderland-born comic George Doonan was also in the company.

By 1908 Chaplin was a new recruit to the nation's premier comedy troupe, Fred Karno's Company of Speechless Comedians. At the Empire Chaplin appeared in *The Football Match*, a sketch in which he played a villain who comes to bribe the star goalkeeper, portrayed by the company's leading comedian, Harry Weldon. During his week at the Empire Charlie celebrated his nineteenth birthday.

A year later, in the week beginning 5 April 1909, the Karno company was back at the Empire with *Mumming Birds*, a sketch which was to transform both Chaplin's career and the history of the cinema. The story of eight inept music hall acts playing to an unappreciative audience of three, the show subsequently toured America where the comedian was spotted by actor and future film producer Mack Sennett. However, Chaplin was not in the *Mumming Birds* company at the Empire. He was still with *The Football Match* but in April 1909 had stepped into Harry Weldon's role of 'Stiffy' the goalkeeper for a performance at Liverpool Olympia. By the end of the year, though, he had switched to *Mumming Birds* and on 6 December 1909, in a performance of the sketch at Hulme Hippodrome, Manchester, Stanley Jefferson made his Karno debut with him, the future Mr Laurel having had to pull out of an appearance at Sunderland Empire to join the company. The following year Laurel left for America with Chaplin.

Stanley Jefferson – the future Stan Laurel.
(Picture courtesy of A.J. Marriot)

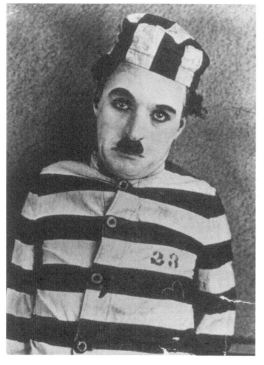

Charlie Chaplin – a Sunderland apprenticeship.

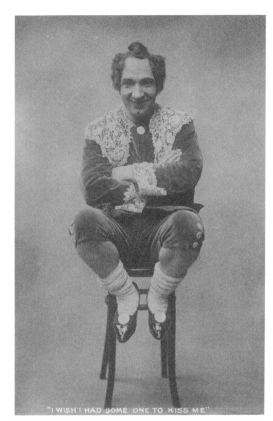

"I WISH I HAD SOME ONE TO KISS ME"

Harry Lauder – in Scots dress and as the page in Cinderella.

Harry Weldon returned to the Empire several times, often with the Karno companies. The first of many Karno visits to Sunderland Empire was in November 1907 with star comedian Fred Kitchen playing the lead role in *The Bailiff*. In December 1912 Chaplin's elder half brother Syd, who also went on to a career in Hollywood, albeit a less illustrious one, took the lead in one of Karno's most ambitious productions, *The Hydro,* which featured a swimming pool on stage.

Stan Laurel and Charlie Chaplin would have been largely unknown to Empire audiences in those days. Harry Lauder, on the other hand, though not yet knighted, was an established star. He was the first big name to play the theatre after Vesta Tilley's opening week. Lauder, who had been given his big break by Frank Allen, came to the Empire on 30 July 1907. It was to be his only visit but he gave the new building his seal of approval. He told the audience, 'I have been in every theatre, music hall and concert hall between Penzance and Inverness, and this is the crowner of them all'.

In subsequent weeks there came a succession of great names. Among them were the comedienne Marie Kendall; the dapper singer of patriotic songs George Lashwood, known as the 'Beau Brummel of the halls'; Eugene Stratton, the leading minstrel or 'coon' performer; Marie Lloyd's second husband Alec Hurley, the king of the Cockney comedians and 'coster' singers; and the actor and singer George Leyton, who with the first house of his opening night established what was, and probably still is, the Empire's record attendance. The *Sunderland Echo* excitedly estimated his audience at 4,000, an alarming 1,000 more than the official capacity.

George Lashwood – the 'Beau Brummel of the halls'.

Less conventional turns in those early weeks were Mariedl, a Tyrolean giantess billed as the world's tallest woman; the eleven-year-old composer, conductor and pianist Max Darewski engaged at the 'stupendous' fee of £250; and a couple of examples of 'living statuary' that presaged the nude shows that were to be such a feature of the theatre's programme in later years. In his assessment of the second of these, *Seldom's Venus*, the *Echo* reviewer wrote, 'It is safe to say that these living reproductions of cold marble cannot fail to satisfy the most exacting critic, whether viewed from the standpoint of art or good taste.' It was clearly a form of entertainment that would have met the stringent requirements of Messrs Thornton and Allen.

Master Darewski, meanwhile, was not allowed to step onto the Empire's respectable stage until there had been a full inquiry into the propriety of having a juvenile – genius or no genius – play the piano late into the night. The Sunderland police court decided he had to be off stage at a time suitable for a small boy and turned down a request that he be allowed to stay up till 10.30 p.m. Nevertheless young Max had time enough to astonish the *Echo*'s reviewer, who wrote, 'He impressed everyone with the fact that his act is not a series of remarkable feats performed by a precocious young trickster, but the natural display of a boy who has been wonderfully and richly inspired'.

As the months wore on the role call of big stars lengthened. There was the eccentric singer and musician G.H. Chirgwin, known as the 'White Eyed Kaffir', who had his face blacked out except for a diamond over his right eye, and the comedy duo Naughton and Gold who were later to form half of the celebrated 'Crazy Gang'. There were the comediennes Marie Loftus and Maidie Scott, the comics Sam Mayo and Ernest Shand, the comedy singer George French and the character comedian and panto dame Neil Kenyon.

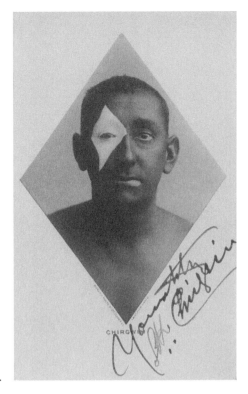

G.H. Chirgwin – the 'White Eyed Kaffir'.

The early Empire more than lived up to its billing as a palace of varieties. Among the speciality acts who graced the stage in the theatre's first decade were whip artists, wood choppers, 'boomerang hat throwers', lasso throwers and a chap who could draw with both hands at the same time. It wasn't enough for them to be skilled merely in their chosen acrobatic diversion – they had to be funny and/or musical as well. There were comedy tumblers, gymnastic comedians and wrestlers who told jokes. The famous Eliotts and Savonas, who appeared several times, were not just trick cyclists, but saxophonists as well.

Several star sportsmen turned to the halls – among them, former world heavyweight boxing champion Bob Fitzsimmons who was at the Empire in May 1909 with his wife to present 'the clever little playlet, *A Man's a Man for A' That'*. Cross-Channel swimmer Jabez Wolfe was on stage in January 1908. Cossack wrestler Ivan Padourny visited Sunderland at the end of September 1907 to challenge any local man to last fifteen minutes with him in the ring. Those who succeeded would receive the princely sum of £15. In the unlikely event of a challenger being able to throw him, a prize of £200 was offered. Since no Wearsider came forward he took on a Bulgarian and a chap from Swindon, as well as an Aberdonian grappler, who lasted seven minutes and fourteen seconds, nine and thirteen minutes, respectively.

In 1909, films of Sunderland football matches began to be shown on the Empire bioscope. The projector was also being used to keep Sunderland in touch with world events, one of which, the French military assault on Moorish forces in Casablanca in the late summer of 1907, was so topical that producers were still working on it when it arrived at the Empire. The footage was not available in its entirety until the second night of its week at the theatre.

Bob Fitzsimmons – heavyweight champion turned actor.

There were animal stars too: Hans, the musical pony and Mascot, the 'highly intelligent horse', in addition to a herd of cricketing elephants who displayed an intelligence that seemed 'almost human', wrote the *Echo*.

Other acts reflected the transport advances of the time. One of the most popular was Harry Tate in his comedy sketch *Motoring*. In March 1908 there was a possibly ill-advised stunt involving 'motoring in mid-air' and in June 1914 a simulated race on stage between a car and a train. Before the war made Zeppelins rather less of an entertainment, the theatre staged a demonstration of a wireless-controlled airship.

A show that would have raised a laugh in the Sunderland of January 1908 and an eyebrow today was The Andos Troupe of *Merry Little Japs*.

By the summer of 1908 the Empire was having a profound effect on its nearest competition. The Livermore Brothers' People's Palace announced in May of that year – when the Empire had not yet been open twelve months – that it would close during the summer. It reopened the following year as a cinema, Hamilton's Flickerless Pictures. Even the grand new King's Theatre on Crowtree Road, in existence a mere eighteen months by the summer of 1908, closed for several weeks to reopen on 24 August under new management and with various improvements.

HARRY TATE.

Harry Tate – motoring comic.

The fact that Sunderland was plunged into industrial depression that summer did not help the fortunes of any theatre, but it was a testament to the strength of the Empire that it was able to weather such an early economic setback.

On 1 July 1908 the Empire celebrated its first birthday. That night General Manager Harry Esden stood on stage to address the audience. The *Echo* reported, 'Mr Esden said he would like to take that opportunity of thanking them on behalf of Mr Thornton very much for their presence and for their generous support during the past twelve months. Notwithstanding the distress in the town and surrounding districts and the trying times they had passed through, he was more than pleased to say the result had been most satisfactory.'

That the Palace had been converted to a cinema was also of course an indication of the increasing power of the moving picture. By September 1912 the *Echo* reported that there were more than a dozen theatres and picture halls in Sunderland, together seating between 18,000 and 19,000 people. The Empire had been the last of the theatres. All the new venues were cinemas. The *Echo* reported that another four cinemas were being built and that 'those in the business are beginning to wonder when the building of new halls is going to stop, and are prophesying that if it goes on much longer, it will lead to disaster in some direction or other'.

4

Home from Home?

Sunderland itself spawned several of the big stars who appeared at the early Empire. The most famous and eccentric was the comedian and singer Mark Sheridan, whose distinctive get-up comprised bell-bottom trousers, an ill-fitting frock coat and a battered stove-pipe hat. Born Fred Shaw in 1864 on Addison Street East, Hendon, Sheridan was described by Charlie Chaplin in his autobiography as 'one of England's foremost comedians'. He began his working life at Laing's shipyard before becoming a programme seller at the Theatre Royal on Bedford Street. Switching from stalls to stage he started as a comedy actor then moved into pantomime and finally branched out as a solo turn in music hall. His speciality was the 'seaside song' and he introduced the most famous of them all, *Oh I Do Like to Be Beside the Seaside*. Another of his hits was *Hello, Hello, Who's Your Lady Friend?*

Sheridan made his Empire debut in June 1910. On a visit in November 1914 he donated his substantial £175 payment to the mayor's local relief fund.

Sheridan was the archetypal tragic comedian – merry on stage, miserable off it. Eventually this balance broke down as he began to lose his hold on an audience. In 1918 he returned to Glasgow, the scene of his earliest success. On 14 January he opened as Napoleon in a revue entitled *Gay Paree,* which he had written. An ambitious undertaking, the play, with a cast of forty-one, had cost £2,000 to produce. Neither the audience nor the critics were as appreciative of the show as they had been of his solo performances. One afternoon Sheridan took a Browning revolver into Kelvingrove Park and shot himself. He was fifty-three years old.

It is entirely fitting that he had not returned to his home town to regain confidence. An *Echo* correspondent, writing in 1930, recalled visiting Sheridan, who lived in London and was often mistaken for a Cockney, in his dressing room at the capital's Oxford Music Hall. On the wall he saw a card which bore the words 'Beware of Sunderland!'. When he asked for an explanation Sheridan told him that 'whenever an artist begins to swank about how well he is going on the stage, we point to the card and threaten to send him there. That settles it!'

He maintained there was no audience so hard to please as 'his ain folk'. His *Echo* obituary pointed out that while he was always a box-office draw in Sunderland, his audiences were often lacking in enthusiasm. Once, during a week at the Palace, he stood at the back of the circle after his performance and watched the rest of the show. Every seat was full. The crowd seemed to be enjoying itself but then, as the punters were leaving, he heard one ask another, 'What do you think of the show?' The reply was, 'Well, it wasn't so bad.' According to the writer of the obituary, Sheridan said in a flash, 'By gosh, that's Sunderland!'

Sheridan's aversion to appearing in Sunderland was such that after his last visit to the Empire he begged Richard Thornton to cancel his remaining contracts to play the theatre. The *Echo* wrote, 'Great indeed was the comedian's delight when he succeeded, and he exclaimed joyfully, "I feel as if I had been given a thousand pounds".'

The Edwardian Empire.

An illuminating exchange of telegrams between Sheridan and Thornton can be seen today framed on a wall at the Empire. The comedian was playing Darlington Hippodrome, but, claiming illness, was hotfooting it back to London rather than keep his following week's booking in Sunderland. Thornton pleads, 'Do make an effort. Would come through with car for you ... only to have you here and keep faith with public.'

Sheridan had no problem with Newcastle audiences, however, and on at least one occasion, he remarked that he would like to select the city for his 'next birthplace'.

Wee Georgie Wood had a happier and longer career than Sheridan. Born above a pawn shop in Jarrow in 1897 but brought up in Sunderland, he became a star before he had reached his teens and remained so into his 60s. Christened George Bamlett, he was 4ft 9in fully grown. As a child he impersonated adults and as an adult he played a small boy. Following an introduction to Vesta Tilley he made his theatre debut at South Shields Empire at the age of nine, and a year later headed the cast of the *Sleeping Beauty* production at the King's Theatre which gave Stan Laurel his big break. In 1910, alternating between comic and tear-jerking songs, and impersonating music hall greats such as Tilley and Marie Lloyd, he made his debut at Sunderland Empire. It was the first of many appearances. Wee Georgie died at his Bloomsbury home in February 1979 at eighty-three years of age.

Mark Sheridan – Sunderland-hating comedian.

Ella Retford, born Eleanor Maude Flanagan on 2 July 1885 on Kingsley Street, Sunderland, made her debut as a dancer in 1900 but later took to singing minstrel songs. Becoming established as a singer, comedienne and actress she appeared at all the major British variety palaces, including the Empire where she first performed in September 1910 and the London Palladium where she was one of the turns on the venue's opening night on Boxing Day of that year.

As well as appearing on variety bills, Ella toured in revues, pantos and the occasional straight play. She also cropped up in films. In pantos, Ella was one of the great principal boys and made her final appearance at the Palace Theatre, Newcastle, in *Mother Goose* in the Christmas season of 1949/50. She collapsed after twelve performances and had to retire from the show. She died in 1962 at seventy-six years of age.

Comedian and actor Ernie Lotinga was born in Sunderland in 1876. The son of a ship broker he made his debut in 1889, and from 1899 appeared with his siblings as one of the 'Brothers Luck'. The brothers came to the Empire in November 1912. He made his London debut in 1901 and his first American appearance on Broadway in 1909. Lotinga was at the Empire as a solo act in June 1913. He was joint top of the bill with the male impersonator and actress Hetty King who was to become his first wife. His most famous character was Jimmy Josser who made the transition from comedy sketch and revue to the big screen in the 1920s and continued to feature in films through the next two decades.

Jake Friedman was known as a 'Dutch comedian' but was born in Sunderland in November 1867. He starred in and produced the Dutch operetta *Happy Holland* at the Empire in December 1908.

Wee Georgie Wood – as an adult and in childhood roles.

Sunderland's glamorous Ella Retford.

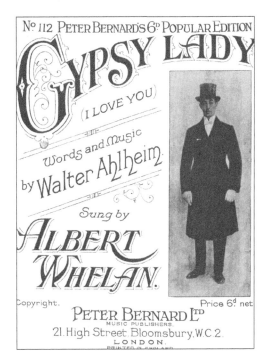

Left: R.G. Knowles – popular everywhere except Sunderland.

Right: Albert Whelan – a fixture on variety bills for years.

A former general dealer and traveller, he had made his first stage appearance at Milburn's Varieties on Gill Bridge Avenue, Sunderland, in 1882. He was subsequently a pupil of music hall legend Charles Coburn, singer of *The Man Who Broke the Bank at Monte Carlo*, and made his London debut in March 1901 as 'the one-man opera'.

Before the Empire opened, Sunderland had a long-established reputation as a hard place to play but that reputation soon spread to the town's grandest venue, helped in no small way by Mr Sheridan, and there it settled during its long years as the town's only professional theatre. Richard Thornton often had to charm a star into completing a week at the theatre. One notable casualty was R.G. Knowles, a Canadian known as the 'express' comedian for his rapid-fire delivery. Knowles was popular around the world. He played long engagements at the Empire on Leicester Square and the Tivoli on the Strand, but when he made his Sunderland Empire debut in April 1911 he had such a bad reception on the first night that he told the management he was going to return to London immediately. Thornton had to plead with him to see out his contract. Eventually Knowles agreed and as the week progressed he had a better time of it but told reporters that his opening-night house had been the worst he had ever experienced and that he would never return to the theatre. He kept his word.

Shortly before the First World War ragtime acts from America became popular but one of those that visited the Empire did not, it seems, meet Wearside's exacting standards and is said to have had a similarly tough time. When the musicians returned to America they met other artists on their way to England and allegedly advised them not to play Sunderland.

The Empire has never lost this image as one of the country's hardest theatres. In the 1980s Irish comedian Frank Carson was asked, 'Are audiences the same the world over?' He answered, 'They are the same the world over … except in Sunderland'.

Above, left and right: G.H. Elliott – one of Sunderland's all-time favourites.

There were, however, many great acts in the theatre's early years who were happy to make many visits. Among the Empire's favourites were comedians Mike B. Whallen, Tom Foy with 'Baley' the donkey, Harry Tate, Bert Weston, Wal Langtry, Scott and Whaley, Ike and Will Scott, the great Gateshead-born comic Jimmy Learmouth (whom the writer J.B. Priestley declared to be the funniest man he ever encountered), the Australian entertainer Albert Whelan, G.H. Elliott, the 'chocolate-coloured coon', and Hetty King, who was married in Sunderland at St Andrew's church, Roker, on 18 June 1918 to Captain Alexander William Lamond. (She was later to become Mrs Ernie Lotinga). Other regular visitors were singer Gertie Gitana (the favourite act of the Empire's architect T.R. Milburn), musical trio Eli, Olga and Elgar Hudson, and ventriloquist 'The Great Coram' with his remote-controlled military dummy 'Jerry', who marched off stage at the climax of the act. Before the First World War, Vesta Tilley returned several times.

A big Empire draw was George Formby senior, who made the first of his visits to the theatre in July 1908. A Lancashire comic, he had always had a troublesome cough. In 1899, he discovered his cough was a symptom of terminal illness. He might have prolonged his life if he'd retired but he had a wife and family to support – including, from 1904, George Formby Jr, whose singing voice was to be remarkably like his father's – and in that cough had found a way to make people laugh. To go with the ailment he created a hapless, dim-witted character 'John Willie' from Lancashire (whose persona George junior later assumed). He died coughing while his audience died laughing. Formby was appearing in a *Jack and Jill* pantomime at Richard

Above, left and right: Hetty King – as gent and lady.

Thornton's Newcastle Empire in February 1921 when he became ill and had to pull out of the show. He died a few days later.

The great Australian singer Florrie Forde, singer of *Pack up Your Troubles in Your Old Kitbag*, made her first visit in June 1915 and returned several times. Making his Empire debut on that same wartime bill was the French comedian Grock. Described by J.B. Priestley in his novel *Lost Empires* as 'the greatest clown after Chaplin', he also became a frequent visitor.

The greatest star of the age, Marie Lloyd, made her first Empire appearance in 1912. She is said to have had trouble with the theatre's audiences but did return – even if it was seven years later – in February 1919. She made a further visit in March 1921, eighteen months before her death.

The Empire stayed open throughout the First World War but could hardly have been oblivious to the conflict. From the beginning the latest war news was shown in film on the Bioscope. In April 1915 the recruiting campaign came to the theatre when Brigadier-General Kelly and Mr McAllan, representative of the Parliamentary Recruiting Committee, gave a patriotic address from the stage. They were accompanied by the Harry Lauder Pipe Band. In June 1915 a full-sized replica of the F7 submarine was on stage in a reenactment of its attack on a German Dreadnought. In August 1916 the Empire screened *Britain Prepared*, 'a stupendous kinematograph review of his majesty's naval and military forces'. A rather less stirring reminder of the war arrived a year later with *The Ten Tommies*, a group of wounded soldiers who performed *Sing Boys Sing*, a show that was incongruously described as a 'happy-go-lucky' novelty.

Above, left and right: George Formby senior – as John Willie and himself.

Left: Gertie Gitana – favourite act of Empire architect T.R. Milburn.

Above, left and right: Florrie Forde –
as a young woman and in later life.

Right: Marie Lloyd – the greatest star
of the age.

Other entertainment during the war ranged from the frothy to the admonitory. A group of 'lady boxers' – female pugilists, not wife-beaters – demonstrated their sport in September 1914. The following September, women took to the water in *Have a Plunge*, the latest 'aquatic' revue from London, featuring thirty-five artists and a large chorus of glamorous swimmers. As the ragtime craze took hold, those acts that had not been warned off in New York poured into the theatre. The brutally direct *7 Spades* featured a syncopated band from Ciro's Supper Club, London, plus 'the greatest combination of ragtime instrumentalists, singers and dancers'.

On the bioscope D.W. Griffith's controversial masterpiece *Birth of a Nation,* with its live orchestral accompaniment, was the big hit in the autumn of 1916. It was retained for a second week.

A warning of the loose morals that came with wartime was delivered by the play *Damaged Goods*, a drama about venereal disease. 'The play has caused much controversy, men of all classes and creeds having been drawn into discussion', ran the advert in the *Echo* during its visit at Christmas in 1917. The play was to retain its shock value when dusted down for the Second World War.

5

The Scene Changes

By the end of the First World War many of the great Victorian entertainers who had visited the theatre in its early years were either dead or in retirement.

In 1920 Vesta Tilley, or Lady de Frece, as she had recently become following Walter's knighthood, bade farewell to the stage, but the palace of varieties she had opened thirteen years earlier could not turn its back on the brave new world of the Jazz Age. The old-style variety bill was for the time being on the wane. The trend was towards the 'intimate revue' which by this time had spread from France to the provincial theatres. The impresario C.B. Cochran and others, chiefly George Grossmith Jr, son of the co-author of *The Diary of a Nobody*, had brought them to the Empire during the First World War but it was in the following decade that they really caught on. The eye-catching titles of the shows were indicative of the dazzling and, as it turned out, illusory, optimism of the times. Among those that mesmerised Sunderland before the General Strike of 1926 were *Designs, Headlights, Rockets, Jingles, Spangles, Sunbeams, Crystals, Mirrors, Visions* and *Radios, Radios, Radios* – most of which starred the comedian George Clarke – and *Zip*, featuring the husband and wife team of Billy Caryll and Hilda Mundy, who developed a routine of on-stage comedy rows following an off-stage tiff.

Later in the decade revue titles were toned down but there was still a taste for glamour, even if it was pure escapism. From London – and from Broadway via London – came the lavish musicals. In 1926 *Rose Marie* and *No, No Nanette* were big successes, as was Gershwin's *Lady Be Good* the following year. Ivor Novello, who was later to corner this market, appeared in 1927 in his first and most successful straight play, *The Rat*. In March 1924, the Danish singer Carl Brisson appeared in his biggest hit, a revival of Lehar's *The Merry Widow*. In 1926 he was back at the Empire in *The Apache*, a show which also featured husband and wife Dorothy Ward and Shaun Glenville, a pairing that clocked up many an Empire success.

The D'Oyly Carte Company, an Empire regular of more recent years, made its first visit in 1922 but opera and Gilbert and Sullivan operetta were not yet a staple of the season even though Sunderland Amateur Operatic Society had begun its long association with the theatre.

From 1843 theatres had been licensed and had had their productions censored by the Lord Chamberlain under the Stage Play Act. Music halls, on the other hand, were not covered by the strictures of that act yet frequently staged dramatic sketches, often of a scurrilous nature, much to the annoyance of the Theatre Managers' Association. In 1907, just in time for the opening of the Empire, a compromise was reached. Music halls and the new variety theatres could stage sketches that had up to a half hour of dialogue. In 1912 music halls came under the jurisdiction of the Lord Chamberlain (which made their entertainment even more respectable) and full-length plays were allowed.

Thereafter they began to appear sporadically at the Empire and it was in the 1920s that they became something of a regular feature. Shakespeare flourished in the mid-1920s, even at Christmas. In 1924, in the week before the Christmas panto, Henry Baynton and his company presented a different Shakespeare play each night. Hundreds had to be turned away at each performance.

Above left and right: Sparring partners Billy Caryll and Hilda Mundy.

Right: Revue star – comedian George Clarke.

Opposite: Vesta Tilley in middle age.

Matinee idol Ivor Novello.

Above, left and right: In and out of costume – Dorothy Ward.

That doughty champion of provincial Shakespeare, Sir Frank Benson, brought the Bard to the Empire in 1925 and there was more Shakespeare in 1928 from Edward Dunston's troupe. The great actor-manager Sir John Martin-Harvey visited the Empire in 1925 and 1927. In the former year he unveiled a plaque in the central library to his old boss, Sir Henry Irving, who had made his professional debut at the Lyceum in Sunderland in 1856.

Towards the end of the 1920s came the Whitehall farces of Ben Travers, *Rookery Nook*, *Thark* and *A Cuckoo in the Nest*, and the thrillers of Edgar Wallace and Arnold Ridley (Private Godfrey in the BBC sitcom *Dad's Army*).

Among the entertainers who appeared at the Empire in the 1920s and early '30s were those who were to become stars of wireless and films. The urbane Jack Buchanan was a frequent visitor in revues and musicals before he became a cinema idol. George Formby Jr, following in the footsteps of his father, was at the theatre in 1925, '27 and '29. Will Hay, the Stockton-born film comedian, played the Empire, as did the comics Robb Wilton, Will Fyffe, George Robey, Jimmy James (also Stockton-born), Sid Field, Sandy Powell, Fred Emney, Tommy Handley, Ted Ray, and Flanagan and Allen.

Gracie Fields, who had earlier appeared at the Empire as a member of a juvenile troupe, disrupted the traffic in Fawcett Street in 1929 when, during a visit to the theatre, she popped along to Binns department store to sign copies of her latest record. Cousins Jimmy Jewell and Ben Warris, who were to become a popular comedy duo, appeared separately at the Empire in 1924 and 1933 respectively. Jewell's future co-star in the sitcom *Nearest and Dearest*, Hylda Baker, a comedienne who strove to have the artistic control and financial clout of her male rivals, made her Empire debut in 1929.

Left: Following in his father's footsteps – George Formby.

Below left: Film comic Will Hay.

Below right: He belonged to Glasgow – Will Fyffe.

The great stage drunk Jimmy James.

Sunderland singing duo Bob and Alf Pearson, who were to become internationally famous, made their Empire debut in the week of 2 June 1930, as did Max Wall, on a bill headed by Wee Georgie Wood, by then in partnership with Dolly Harmer, who acted as his stage mother.

Bob was born in August 1907, Alf in June 1910. As teenagers they joined an amateur concert party, the *Blue Boys*, with Bob at the piano and Alf standing alongside. The brothers worked for the family plastering firm, which relocated to Surrey at Easter 1928. It was there that the boys' mother entered them in a national talent competition run by Columbia Records. They won it, received a recording contract and had their music played by Christopher Stone on the BBC. They made their London debut at the Hippodrome, Greenwich in 1929, earning 30 shillings as one of the turns on a Friday night cine-variety bill. Broadcasting dates followed on Saturday Night Music Hall. After a date back in the North East in a charity matinee at Gateshead Empire, they embarked on a tour of the Thornton circuit. By the time they reached Sunderland Empire they were up-and-coming stars and made celebrity appearances at Binns and at Lloyd's music shop in Bridge Street, autographing copies of their records. It was the first of many Empire appearances for the duo. Bob died in 1985 but, at the time of writing, Alf is still living in Surbiton, Surrey, and is active in the Water Rats show business charity.

Among the other Sunderland men who appeared at the Empire in this period were the comedians George Doonan and George Jackley.

Known as 'The Indignant Comedian', Jackley too had an international career. His father Nathan had been a circus performer who ran a troupe called the 'Jackley Wonders'. A 'Jackley Trio' had been on one of the Empire's first variety bills. In panto he achieved his biggest success at the Lyceum in London where he appeared every Christmas for twelve years.

Above, left and right: George - later Sir George – Robey, in two comic guises.

Left: 'My brother and I' – Sunderland's Bob and Alf Pearson in later life on a return to Sunderland Empire.

Max Wall – Empire debut in 1930.

'Life and soul of the party' – Sunderland's George
Doonan.

Above and left:
Richard Thornton
and wife with their
gypsy caravan and
chalet.

Doonan meanwhile had made his first stage appearance in 1904 and, as we have seen, toured in Casey's Circus with Charlie Chaplin. He made his solo debut in 1909 and went on to appear in South Africa, Australia, New Zealand and the USA. One of the first comedians to adopt smart lounge suits as opposed to evening wear as stage attire, he was billed as 'The Life and Soul of the Party'.

It was not just the retirement of Vesta Tilley and the demise of music hall that in the 1920s severed the Empire's links with its early years. The decade also saw the death of Richard Thornton and Frank Allen. Thornton died on 21 February 1922 at the age of eighty-three and was succeeded as managing director by Colonel J.J. Gillespie.

At his death Thornton was worth more than £100,000. The former colliery pick-sharpener had risen to a grand lifestyle with an imposing home in Gosforth, Newcastle. However, in his final years he had chosen not to live in the house itself but in a large Norwegian chalet in the grounds. Thornton, who also owned a gypsy caravan, had taken a liking to the wooden home on a trip to Scandinavia and had arranged for it to be shipped in sections to Newcastle. In her autobiography Vesta Tilley does not mention Sunderland Empire but she does reminisce about Thornton's eccentric living arrangements. She says that when the great theatre owner moved into the chalet he let his house. This led to trouble with the neighbours who wanted the chalet removed since it overlooked their gardens. With typical aplomb Thornton contacted the owners of the freehold for the terrace and bought all the houses. He then gave those tenants who objected to his chalet notice to leave. But he was also a generous man, leaving money in his will to many of his employees.

His obituary in the *Sunderland Echo* referred to him as the 'Napoleon of the music hall world' since he had risen from such lowly origins to become 'the doyen of the music hall business'.

An obituary in the North East-based *Illustrated Chronicle* of Wednesday 22 February 1922 lamented, 'the gap left by the passing of "The Guvnor" will be difficult to fill.'

6

Alone in the Spotlight

The early 1930s were a bleak time for the North East in the grip of economic depression. What cash there was went on essentials and the theatre was not one of them. Those who could afford to go out for an evening were now more likely to visit one of the many cinemas, but even these were not safe from the threat of closure. It soon became apparent that the region could support little more than a handful of theatres. In response to the recession the big theatre and cinema chains merged and their less profitable operations were shut down. In 1932 Moss Empires was taken over by Gaumont-British Film Corporation (which had already absorbed another amalgamation, the General Theatres Corporation headed by Sunderland's George Black, whose father had opened the town's first cinema) and the following year its northern subsidiary group – Richard Thornton's North East Circuit – was wound up. Sunderland Empire became fully a part of Moss Empires. Richard Reed, who had married an adopted daughter of Richard Thornton, and had become general and booking manager for the Thornton theatres, was appointed supervisor of the Midlands, Northern and Scottish Moss Empires. In the spring of 1932 the 'kine-variety' policy which he introduced in Sunderland – films, plus a variety show on a rolling programme from 2 p.m. to 10.30 p.m., six days a week – was adopted throughout the Moss circuit in the north and it seemed to be a winning formula to keep some of the theatres open.

But by the end of 1933 Sunderland's Avenue and Theatre Royal, both of which had been operating as cinemas, were closed. The Avenue was later taken over by Vaux Breweries and turned into a bottling hall. It was demolished in 2001 with the rest of the brewery. The Royal reopened as a cinema in 1940 and later became, successively, a bingo hall and night club. It was demolished in 1996.

In South Shields in 1934, Richard Thornton's Empire was converted into a cinema while his Theatre Royal became a shop. Part of the façades of both theatres can still be seen above Shoefayre and Marks & Spencer. In Newcastle the Hippodrome and Theatre Royal closed, albeit temporarily in the case of the latter. In Gateshead and Newcastle alone, 120 theatre musicians, technicians and administrators were thrown on to the dole.

Of the Empires it seemed that only Newcastle was safe. By the autumn of 1932 kine-variety had been abandoned at Sunderland Empire and the following spring it was strongly rumoured that the theatre would shut down. However, one of Gaumont-British Film Corporation's main intentions in taking over the Moss organisation had been to prevent the Empires from converting to film and competing with its own chain of cinemas. Sunderland Empire was allowed to stay open to concentrate on what it was designed to do – present live entertainment. But first it had four months off for redecoration.

It reopened in 1933 with *Women of the World*, starring singer, dancer and actress Janice Hart. Live entertainment continued for the rest of the decade except for two more summer breaks, in 1934 and 1935. During the latter the theatre was decorated once again and new stage lighting installed. It was also shut down for a week in August 1936 for electrical work. It was at this time that microphones were introduced into most variety halls, making for a more intimate style of entertainment.

Nat Jackley – a comic from a
Sunderland entertainment dynasty.

At the Empire, revues and the occasional week of variety were the standard fare with repertory theatre taking over each summer from 1936 to 1940.

Sunderland's Ernie Lotinga returned, performing his Jimmy Josser sketches that by now had been seen on the big screen. Ella Retford was also back on the Empire boards and Nat Jackley made his debut, following in the family footsteps. Like Charlie Chaplin, Nat, born in 1909, began as a member of the 'Eight Lancashire Lads'. He moved on to a double act with his sister Joy, then joined forces with comedian Jack Clifford. He started out as Clifford's straight man but discovered he was funnier and so they swapped roles. After going solo Nat understudied Fred Astaire in *Lady Be Good* in the West End, topped the bill at the London Palladium and appeared in three Royal Variety Performances. He later became a great panto dame, appearing in his final Christmas show at the Tyne Theatre, Newcastle, in 1984. He died in 1988. Joy Jackley also worked in a double act with brother Dave, a singer and dancer who became a straight man to comedian Jack Radcliffe. He was later a company manager and was in that role with The Mating Game at the Empire in 1976 when film comedian Sid James died on stage.

At the Empire in the 1930s many of the variety bills and revues had a radio theme and featured stars of the airwaves such as Empire stalwarts Tommy Handley and Sandy Powell, Canadian Carroll Levis and his BBC *Discoveries* talent show, Elsie and Doris Waters, and Ben Lyon and Bebe Daniels.

Above left: 'Can you 'ear me, Mother?'
Comic Sandy Powell.

Above right: The Street Singer – Arthur Tracy.

Left: Talent-spotter Carroll Levis.

Opposite: Elsie and Doris Waters.

Bandleaders Ambrose, Roy Fox, Lew Stone, Jack Hylton.

In January 1937 future television talent-spotter Hughie Green, who was to fight a long and acrimonious legal battle in the 1950s with Carroll Levis over the talent-spotting copyright, appeared with his Famous Boys and Girl Gangsters in *Radio Rhythm*. Green, the godson of former Empire regular, comic Harry Tate, was then seventeen and had been touring with his own show since the age of thirteen. Another teen star, singer Betty Driver, the future Betty Turpin in television soap *Coronation Street*, featured on several Empire variety bills.

It was not just BBC stars who provided the entertainment. Performers from Radio Luxembourg and Radio Normandy also visited the Empire – among them was Arthur Tracy, the busking American billed as The Street Singer, who became a big hit in this country by having his music broadcast from continental stations.

In the 1930s dance bands moved into variety theatres and became as popular an attraction there as they had been in the hotels and ballrooms. Among those at the Empire were orchestras led by Harry Roy, Jack Payne, Jack Hylton, Ambrose, Roy Fox, Lew Stone, and the 24-stone

American xylophonist Teddy Brown, who was to become a firm favourite at the Empire. Another popular mallet man to appear several times at the theatre was the American musician and knockabout comedian Will Mahoney, whose speciality was playing a giant xylophone with hammers attached to his feet. Peg Leg Bates, conversely, made a virtue of his lack of leg power. Despite being one-legged he was a great dancer, as he showed at the Empire in 1936. In rather more conventional style, trumpeter Nat Gonella, a star of Lew Stone's band, brought his Georgians on their first British tour in 1935. Ambrose led his Octet featuring Vera Lynn at the Empire in May 1939.

From Hollywood came film stars Anna May Wong, who was in Britain to make the movies *Chu Chin Chow* and *Java Head*, and cowboy actor Tom Mix with his horse Tony. In April 1939 the Empire saw a spectacular music and comedy show from the States which featured The Mills Brothers, The Three Stooges and Fats Waller. While they were in Sunderland, The Mills Brothers and Fats were guests at the stag night of Richard Reed Jr, son of the theatre's general manager.

Left and below: Mallet men –
Will Mahoney and Teddy Brown.

Opposite: Peg Leg Bates.

Above: Cowboy star Tom Mix and his horse Tony on stage at the Empire.

Opposite below: Fats Waller and the Mills Brothers backstage at the Empire for the stag night of Richard Reed Jr (centre left). Theatre boss Richard Reed is centre right.

Right: Empire stalwart Frank E. Franks.

The first repertory season in 1936 was put together by Alfred Denville. He appealed to the Sunderland public to support his attempt to bring 'legitimate' theatre to the town. Drama survived – there was another repertory season the following summer – but Denville's residency did not. That year's troupe was the Donal Gilbert Repertory Company. In the summer of 1938 film star John Stuart headed the cast each week for the King and McCormick Company.

Rather more popular were the dancing girls – The 15 Dancing Babes, The Thrillables and The 16 English Belles – who were a leggy presence in most of the revues and variety shows. Also big draws were the circuses and midget shows that occasionally supplanted them.

A regular name in the pantos and variety bills of the period was that of Frank E. Franks. He appeared at the Empire more times than anyone else in the theatre's first forty years. Born Francis Kane in Hebburn in 1892, he worked in the shipyards and the mines, entertaining at local venues before doing his nightshift. His colliery overseer encouraged him to switch to the stage full-time. At his first professional appearance at the Imperial Cinema, Bill Quay, on the Tyne, he was spotted by Richard Thornton. In 1921 he married male impersonator and panto principal Ruth Kitson from Langley Moor, Durham, who used the stage name 'Gene Boyne'. They were to appear together often in the Empire shows that Frank wrote and produced.

Frank appeared in two Royal Command Performances, but was best known in the North East. Fred Green, who was a doorman at the Empire for fifty years from 1931, said Franks was his favourite entertainer in all those years. In 1987 Fred told me, 'Some of the people who have appeared here have had hearts of gold, but I think the greatest of them all was Frank E. Franks. When he was packing them in here he used to take me along the queue and pick out the kids with no shoes and raggy clothes and he used to fit them out.' Franks retired in 1950 after an 8,000-mile farewell tour of his thirty favourite theatres, but made several brief comebacks. He died in April 1974 at the age of eighty-two in his home on Chapel Hill Road, Peterlee.

7

A Theatre At War

On 3 September 1939 Sunderland Empire was closed on government orders. As part of regulations announced within minutes of the declaration of war all places where people might congregate in large numbers, with the exception of churches, were shut down until further notice. That Sunday the Empire was thirteen weeks into a seventeen-week season by Sunderland Repertory Company, featuring film actor John Stuart. The latest production, Arnold Ridley's *Ghost Train,* had finished the night before. The company dispersed and the Empire was out of action for a fortnight.

The closure of theatres brought immediate protests. George Bernard Shaw was among those who pointed out that during the First World War they had played an essential role in providing entertainment for soldiers on leave. On Saturday 16 September it was announced that they would be allowed to reopen, provided they were closed by 10 p.m. each night.

As soon as news broke, the indefatigable Frank E. Franks set to work. Between 12.30 p.m. that day and the first house at 5.40 p.m. on Monday 18 September, he created *Take Cover*, described as 'A Bang up-to-the-Minute Variety Revue with a Big Cast of London Artists'. The show poked fun at the Air Raid Precautions and saw the lighter side of evacuations and the blackouts. The invitation was to 'come and laugh it off'.

The war was to give a boost to theatrical fortunes and the Empire was part of the chain which dominated the business during that period. Thanks to the demand for manpower in the forces and the factories, unemployment was wiped out. Wages were relatively generous and the only luxury to be purchased was a night of glamour and escapism at the theatre or cinema. There was a demand for manpower in show business too, particularly when many of the younger entertainers were on duty abroad. Old stars, such as music hall legend Harry Champion, came out of retirement to enjoy an Indian summer of nostalgia. In Champion's case it proved to be a brief one. He died in January 1942 following a nervous breakdown caused by overwork.

Although it had a steady supply of acts, the Empire was not exempt from rationing in other areas. Makeup was hard to come by and so was the soap to remove it. Actors and variety artists had a concession when it came to costumes but they failed in an attempt to get their soap ration increased. And even if they had the costumes and props, they experienced difficulty getting them from theatre to theatre since railway baggage was restricted to 100lbs per person.

In the blackout the Empire could no longer light up the sky along High Street West and from 1944 it was, like other theatres, prohibited from using electricity or fuel for heating between mid-April and the end of October. But the theatre did stay open, a fact that was not lost on one William Joyce, the infamous 'Lord Haw-Haw', who chillingly referred to the Empire in the detailed British broadcasts he made for the German propaganda machine.

During air raids the audience was given the opportunity to leave for the shelters but frequently stayed put. The only interruption came from the trials of wartime travel. On Monday 9 January 1940, for what was reckoned to be the first time in the Empire's thirty-three-year history,

Right: Playwright and actor Arnold Ridley, writer of perennial favourite *The Ghost Train*, in wartime guise as a member of the *Dad's Army* cast.

Below: Jesse Challons – Empire manager for more than two decades. He would 'defy' the audience to come in, said comic Robb Wilton.

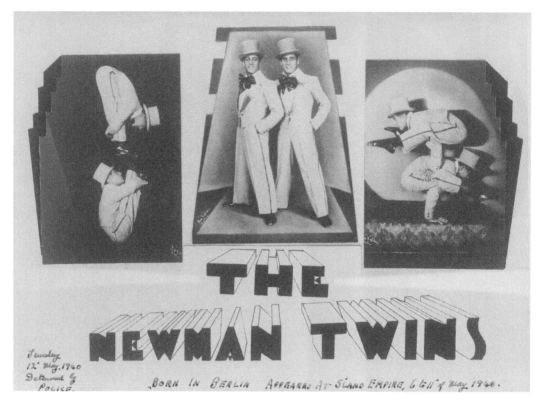

The Newman Twins – arrested after their week in Sunderland.

the show did not go on. The cast of the revue *It's a Wow* left Manchester at 9 a.m. on Sunday 8 January and reached the Empire the following night but not in time for even the second house. The theatre's manager, Jesse Challons, told the *Sunderland Echo*, 'I have known nothing like it in my long career with theatres. I have had floods, fires, fights and escaping wild animals, but this breaks new ground. Never have I seen a touring company reach their destination so worn out.'

The comedy contortionists and acrobats, the Newman Twins, had no trouble reaching the Empire but had considerable trouble leaving it, or at least leaving it as they would have wished. The brothers Max and Gabriel Neuman had been born in Berlin. On Sunday 12 May 1940, at the end of a week at the theatre on a bill that included bandleader Henry Hall and comedian Jimmy James, they were detained by police and taken to an internment camp with other 'enemy aliens'.

In March 1943 the cast of *Damaged Goods*, the play about venereal disease that had also played at the theatre during the First World War, had to be rescued from the Empress Hotel on Union Street, which was badly damaged in a night of heavy bombing. Two months later the Empire itself was showered with debris when a land mine fell behind the Dun Cow pub, demolishing a warehouse on what is now the car park between the theatre and old fire station.

The war brought with it shows that might have had the effect of dropping a bombshell among Sunderland Empire's Edwardian founders. Their unease would have been justified but for the wrong reasons. The nude shows that arrived in the 1940s, which had been pioneered by

Guardian of public morals –
Alderman Joseph Hoy.

Sunderland's Ernie Lotinga, who gave their biggest star, Phyllis Dixey, her big break, were rather staid affairs that strove for artistic respectability. Nude shows did however help bring about the death of variety and variety theatres like the Empire when they spread to epidemic proportions in the 1950s. It was a need to keep off-duty servicemen entertained that led to a relaxation of the strict rules of theatrical propriety in this respect, although the Lord Chamberlain did not issue a licence for lewdness. Much like the 'living statues' of the Empire's early days, the nudes had to stay perfectly still on stage and were instructed to have certain areas of their bodies discreetly disguised.

Phyllis Dixey had appeared down the bill of a Lotinga show at the Empire in 1934 but it was fronting her own entertainment, *Eve Takes A Bow*, that she arrived at the theatre in March 1940. Dixey and her girls would pose for a few seconds, their bodies covered in a gauze gown that was invisible to the audience, before dashing in darkness to the wings. Chief Constable George Cook and Alderman Joseph Hoy of the Watch Committee sat at the back of the stalls every Monday night and if there had been the merest suggestion of impropriety they would have had the show stopped. The war's favourite nude, the celebrated 'Jane' cartoon of the *Daily Mirror*, was fleshed out for the stage and appeared at the Empire during the conflict, as did Gaston and Andree, a male and female nude act who helped maintain morale in such shows as *Artistes and Models* at the theatre in September 1944.

At the other end of the spectrum of decency were the wartime concerts of classical music with Dame Myra Hess and the London Symphony Orchestra, Sadler's Wells Opera, Richard Tauber, Rawicz and Landauer, D'Oyly Carte, the Carl Rosa Opera Company, and the National Philharmonic Orchestra with Webster Booth and Anne Ziegler.

Something for everyone – Gaston & Andree.

Forces' sweetheart Vera Lynn.

Above, left and right: Wartime pin-ups – Evelyn Taylor and Cynthia Rawson.

There were inevitable wartime references in many of the shows. The first panto of the war featured '16 Wearside Wee Evacuees', Tom Moss and Beryl Reid appeared in *We're in the Army Now*, Frank E. Franks headed *The Home Guard's Parade* and Ernie Lotinga brought his review *The Air Force*. Forces' sweetheart Vera Lynn headed a variety bill in April 1942. Among the other wartime pin-ups to appear at the theatre were Evelyn Taylor, star act on the exotic-sounding bill *Une Nuit Exitante* in August 1940, and pianist Cynthia Rawson, who appeared with Tommy Fields (brother of Gracie) and South Shields comic Albert Burdon in variety in May 1943. Tap dancer and comedian Frank Formby, George Jr's younger brother, followed in the family tradition at the Empire, appearing in *Laughter Cavalcade* in March 1940.

Among the stage versions of radio shows that came out on tour were *Garrison Theatre*, starring Jack Warner and featuring the little-known Ernie Wise, at the Empire in July 1942, and *Happidrome*, with Cecil Fredericks, Robbie Vincent and Harry Korriss, and *Ramsbottom and Enoch and me*, which came for two weeks in December of that year.

Band leader Joe Loss made his first appearance at the theatre in March 1940 with Monte Rey and Hartlepool vocalist Chick Henderson. It was to be one of Chick's last performances before his mysterious death during the war. The versatile G.S. Melvin, one of the greats of variety with his comic characters, quick changes and soft-shoe dancing, was on the same bill. Curiously Melvin had been billed to appear on the Empire's first night in 1907 but gets no mention in the *Sunderland Daily Echo*'s detailed review of the occasion. It is possible that he pulled out at the last minute and was replaced by comedian Charlie Kay who is mentioned by the *Echo* but is not on the bill. Melvin, who went on to make many Empire appearances, died tragically just after the end of the Second World War when he was drowned in a flooded reach of the Thames near his home at Kingswood Creek.

Above left: Tommy Fields, comedian brother of Gracie.

Above right: South Shields comic Albert Burdon.

Left: Following in the family tradition at the Empire – Frank Formby.

Right: Monte Rey – Glaswegian singer of romantic song.

Below, left and right: G.S. Melvin – in and out of character.

Roma Beaumont.

West End plays, such as *Arsenic and Old Lace* and *No Orchids for Miss Blandish*, were a popular Empire attraction during the war, but the biggest hits of the period were the glamorous musicals, particularly Ivor Novello's *The Dancing Years*, starring Novello himself, Muriel Barron and Roma Beaumont. The show was rapturously received in January 1941. The following year Roma married Alfred Black, son of Sunderland's George Black, the managing director of Moss Empires. They met while Roma was starring with Vic Oliver, Pat Kirkwood and Carol Lynn (the future wife of Lord Bernard Delfont) in *Black Velvet*, a wartime morale booster staged by George with Alfred as one of the producers.

When the war ended it was at the Empire and other local venues that many Wearsiders heard the official announcement. The *Sunderland Echo* of Tuesday 8 May 1945 reported that the reaction of audiences around the town was a sober one.

'There was little vociferous demonstration. The atmosphere was rather one of deep and proud satisfaction and audiences stood stiffly to attention while the National Anthem was played.'

8

Age of Austerity

Sunderland Empire's fortieth birthday in 1947 was not an entirely happy occasion. An article in the *Sunderland Echo* of 30 June of that year praised the theatre's managers for booking nothing but the 'best available', but castigated audiences for giving the place a bad reputation. Support from the public was often 'sadly lacking', said the writer. He was largely referring to variety shows but the situation was even more serious for drama and ballet. In the immediate post-war years even West End hit plays – *The Winslow Boy* and *Charley's Aunt* among them – had a sticky time at the theatre. Drama producers might have been well advised to stay clear of Sunderland altogether. The newly created Arts Council sent out productions for a few years running to venues as diverse as Sunderland's Drama Club's converted church hall at The Royalty and the Miners' Welfare Hall in Houghton-le-Spring but there was a lack of support from Wearside audiences.

In 1946 the dancers of the Metropolitan Ballet attracted a paltry crowd to the Empire and left feeling disheartened. A couple of years later it took an appeal in the columns of the *Sunderland Echo* to whip up support for the visit to the theatre by International Ballet. 'If cultural entertainment is to find a footing in Sunderland, then Wearside apathy must be banished', wrote *Looker-On*.

By March 1949 the same column was putting the case for a Sunderland concert hall since so many theatre and ballet companies faced with the problem of filling the Empire were performing in the town's schools. At the same time the Empire was losing its dance bands, which had been a popular attraction in the 1930s and the war years, to the dance halls. These were boom years for the Seaburn Hall, The Rink in Park Lane and Sunderland Greyhound Stadium, where townsfolk could do more than merely look and listen to local favourites, such as Al Flush and national stars Harry Gold and Oscar Rabin. They were also flocking in record numbers to the cinemas where occasionally they would be treated to a personal appearance by a star. Keiron Moore, who had starred with Sunderland's Christine Norden in *Mine Own Executioner*, visited the town in February 1947. Sunderland-born film actor Gibb McLaughlin meanwhile returned for a celebrity visit in October 1948.

On the national stage the late 1940s are considered a boom time for variety with the arrival of such performers and writers as Spike Milligan and Peter Sellers. But as late as 1948 the *Sunderland Echo* was complaining that the stage was being blocked by tired old turns. It also lamented that when such artists left for that theatre in the sky there were few new stars to replace them.

In 1948 Randolph Sutton, G.H. Elliott, Gertie Gitana, Ella Shields and Talbot O'Farrell returned to the Empire on the first tour of the music hall nostalgia show *Thanks for the Memory*. Produced by Miss Gitana's husband, Don Ross, it marked Gertie's first appearance in Sunderland since a farewell performance sixteen years earlier. The *Echo*'s reviewer did, in the event, give these old turns a favourable write-up. In September 1950, however, husband and wife Dorothy Squires and Billy Reid had a less favourable reception. They walked off stage after constant heckling

Sunderland film star Christine
Norden.

Film star Trevor Howard signing autographs at Sunderland's Havelock Cinema.

Above left: Dorothy Squires – heckled.

Above right: Bennie Hill – slow handclapped.

Above left: Frankie Howerd – bright young star.

Above right: Hypnotist Peter Casson – entrancing Empire audiences for decades.

Left: Singer and actor Allan Jones – 'greeted with shrieks of delight'.

Above left: Marqeez, exotic Folies Bergere dancer at the Empire in May 1949.

Above right: Felix Mendelssohn – London-born Hawaiian at the Empire in October 1947.

from the gallery at the second house of their last night. Sunderland's reputation as a hard place to play was still in boisterous good health. In April 1951 the twenty-seven-year-old Benny Hill arrived as straight man to comic and musician (and future *On the Buses* television sitcom star) Reg Varney. Hill rashly tried out a solo act but was afflicted by stage fright, dried up in front of that unforgiving audience and was subjected to a slow hand clap. He sloped off stage and was sick in his dressing room sink. After an argument with the theatre manager he was dropped from the show.

One young star who did win the approval of the *Sunderland Echo* and the Empire audience was Frankie Howerd. The *Echo* of 3 May 1948 referred to him as 'the most talked-of young man since (Sunderland star footballer) Len Shackleton arrived'. Howerd had been a hit the previous week in *Ta-Ra-Ra Boom-De-Ay* and returned in triumph the following September and again in November 1949. Another big star of the future was Julie Andrews, who was in twice-nightly variety at the Empire with her parents Ted and Barbara in May 1949. That year also saw the first visit to the Empire of hypnotist Peter Casson who was to be a fixture on the provincial circuit for decades.

The late 1940s were marked by an influx of American stars. The man responsible was Val Parnell, who in 1945 had succeeded Sunderland's George Black as head of Moss Empires. He brought Danny Kaye to the flagship London Palladium in 1948 and in his wake there came to the Empire a wave of big names from across the Atlantic, among them Chico Marx, the Nicholas Brothers, dancer and film actress Peggy Ray, and singer Allan Jones, whose songs were 'greeted with shrieks of delight', wrote the *Echo* reviewer. Appearing with Jones (father of singer Jack Jones) was his wife Irene Hervy.

Molly Moselle, who disappeared
from the Empire in 1949.

The perennial successes at the Empire were the musicals and novelty shows. Among the former were Ivor Novello's *Perchance to Dream*, *Glamorous Nights* and *The Dancing Years*. Among the latter were *Hold Your Breath* which featured an underwater display on stage by frogmen and even a sub-aquatic striptease by the lovely Marree. *Way out West*, meanwhile, at the Empire in September 1949, starred Big Bill Campbell, whose singing company, including various braves and squaws, recreated wild west scenes on stage. Ice shows were also a big draw in the late 1940s.

It was, however, the real-life Empire drama of Molly Moselle that grabbed the biggest headlines of the period. It is a story that has enthralled Sunderland ever since.

On the afternoon of 14 January 1949, the thirty-three-year-old stage manager of Ivor Novello's *The Dancing Years* left her lodgings in Eden Street just behind the theatre. She told her landlady, the Empire wardrobe mistress Ethel Smart, that she was going to buy a birthday card for Barry Sinclair, the show's leading man. She never returned.

Molly was said to have been depressed. She had had affairs with comedian Bunny Doyle and a Sheffield businessman Walter Hattersley and both had recently broken up. In 1957 Bunny Doyle died and left her £200 and a car in his will but no one came forward to claim these. The Sunderland police file on Molly is still open. The final entry refers to the badly decomposed torso of an unidentified woman found in the River Wear in 1960.

9

Sex, TV and Rock 'n' Roll

Before the watershed of the mid-1950s twice-nightly variety had one last flourish at the Empire. Among the entertainers were such new faces as Terry Thomas, Harry Secombe, Ken Dodd, Harry Worth (who initially appeared as a ventriloquist) and Chic Murray. Tony Hancock visited the Empire in August 1951 on a bill topped by Bob and Alf Pearson. He returned to the theatre in February 1952 with the stage version of the radio hit *Educating Archie*, starring ventriloquist Peter Brough.

Ken Dodd, who has now clocked up the longest Empire career of any entertainer, first appeared on 4 October 1954 on his second professional date, having made his debut a few days earlier at Nottingham Playhouse. The following May he returned to the Empire theatre on a bill topped by trumpeter Eddie Calvert. This time he made more of an impact on the *Echo* critic, who wrote, 'Ken Dodd is a comedian of dreadful demeanour. He is like Peter Ustinov dressed as a clown imitating Maurice Chevalier. The total effect is affrighting and convulsing'.

Among the other new entertainers were Bruce Forsyth, who appeared at the foot of a variety bill in March 1956, and Des O'Connor, who scored an Empire hit in June the following year. O'Connor's comedy nemesis Eric Morecambe had by the early '50s teamed up with Ernie Wise and the duo began to crop up on Empire bills, although the big comedy draws at the beginning of the decade were such musical mayhem acts as Dr Crock and his 'Crackpots' and Syd Millward and his 'Nitwits'.

The new generation of singers included Ruby Murray, Jimmy Young, Kirk Stevens, Frankie Vaughan, David Whitfield, Lee Lawrence and Ronnie Hilton. Ronnie Ronalde, who was a virtuoso bird mimic and whistler or 'siffleur', as well as a singer, was a frequent visitor to the Empire. His early appearances were with Steffani's Silver Songsters.

A singer and comedian from a slightly earlier generation, Issy Bonn, also made many appearances despite suffering the Sunderland audience at its worst: on a 1940s visit he was subjected to anti-Semitic barracking.

Entertainers such as Vic Oliver and Sunderland's Bob and Alf Pearson, who had visited the Empire before the Second World War, continued to draw big crowds as did inevitably, in the breaks from variety, the Ivor Novello musicals and new West End shows, notably *Carousel* starring Edmund Hockridge. Circuses were also hugely popular.

Local acts following in the Pearson brothers' footsteps were Sunderland-born impressionist Eddie Arnold (not to be confused with American country singer Eddy Arnold) – who was to appear elsewhere with such legends as Bob Hope, Dean Martin and Jerry Lewis – The Five Smith Brothers from Tyneside and Wearside's own legendary comedian Bobby Thompson.

Bobby, born in Penshaw in 1911, was a former miner and labourer whose stories of debt and dole were based on personal experiences. He topped the bill at the Empire for the first time in July 1955 and starred in the theatre's panto later that year and in 1956.

Left: The sartorial Terry-Thomas at the Empire. He sported a fresh carnation every day, but this one was drooping.

Below: Frankie Vaughan meets his Empire admirers.

Above left: Ronnie Hilton, with a young fan on a '50s visit to Sunderland.

Above right: Issy Bonn – a perennial at the Empire despite an occasionally hostile reception.

While appearing in the *Mother Goose* panto of 1961 he and his family stayed in a caravan in the Empire car park after being evicted from their council house in Great Lumley, Bobby and wife Phyllis having drunk the rent money. At the Empire the other stars on the bill would come out to the caravan to meet the Thompson family. Sons Michael and Keith remember the singer Craig Douglas, who starred with Bobby and Nat Mills in *Mother Goose*, sharing a sumptuous meal of 'Hoggett's' potato crisps spread with 'Shippam's' paste in Bobby's mobile home. The crisps and paste had been supplied by the manufacturers in return for mentions in the show. His third billing in that production was one of his few successes during a profound slump in fortunes brought on by a disastrous attempt at television comedy on the new *Tyne Tees* television channel.

In a life of tempestuous ups and downs Bobby was to have a continuing association with his home town theatre. He loved the Empire, says Keith. For many years it was one of the places where he could indulge his twin passions for drink and chorus girls. His last Empire appearance was at a charity show shortly before his death in 1988.

In that July 1955 bill Bobby appeared with The Merry Magpies who included Gene Patton, a whistling, dancing comic from Hetton-le-Hole, who had worked with and understudied Sunderland's Ernie Lotinga. Gene, whose real name was James Patton Elliott, was the father of The Chuckle Brothers and the Patton Brothers. He played Widow Twankey to Bobby's Wishee Washee in the 1956 *Aladdin*.

A performer with an unusual act, who was to settle in Sunderland, appeared on a December 1954 bill. He was Ken Wheal, better known as Checker Wheel, the 'Fred Astaire of roller skating'. Meanwhile from abroad came Billy Daniels, Guy Mitchell, zither player Anton Karas, Al Martino, Stubby Kaye, and Laurel and Hardy, who visited the Empire in March 1952 and February 1954.

Checker Wheel in black-face, rolling-skating routine.

Above left: Sunderland comic Bobby Thompson.

Above right: Al Martino with his wife who flew to be with him at the Empire.

Right: Stubby Kaye, star of Hollywood's *Guys and Dolls.*

Stan Laurel and Oliver Hardy at Sunderland Empire with Benny Barron in 1952. (Picture courtesy of A.J. Marriot)

Father John Caden, who in 1952 became the Empire's first Catholic chaplain, met the great comedy duo on one of his first trips back stage. He recalls, 'I was trembling as I knocked at their dressing room door. They were the biggest stars in the world to come out on tour at that time and I found them utterly charming. If I'd been the Pope, they couldn't have made more fuss of me. They left a lasting impression on me as huge stars who were yet so humble and unassuming.'

'As I was leaving I turned to Oliver Hardy and said, "I feel very lucky, you've given so much laughter to me and other people". And he smiled and kind of twiddled his tie in that Oliver Hardy way and said, "That's very gracious, father", and immediately changed the subject'.

On the 1952 visit Stan was reunited with seventy-year-old Benny Barron from Sunderland, who had been with him in the *Sleeping Beauty* panto at the King's Theatre in the town forty-five years earlier. Benny turned up back stage with his son Billy, a trumpeter in the Empire orchestra, and they reminisced about the good old days, with Stan also recalling an appearance at the Villiers Institute in Sunderland. Billy reckons Stan picked up many of his facial expressions, and his trick of 'crying' from Benny, whom Laurel had seen many times in a comedy double act with Jack Graham.

After the 1954 visit Stan had a less happy exchange of views with another of his *Sleeping Beauty* colleagues, Trixie Wyatt, also from Sunderland. In 1952 Laurel and Hardy had gone down well with the Empire audience and the *Sunderland Echo* reviewer. Two years later the *Echo* critic suggested they had become an anachronism and they played to far from full houses. Stan wrote to Trixie, ' ... it was a miserable week, was glad to get out of it.'

In and out of character – Shaun Glenville, who returned to the Empire on a nostalgia trip.

Contemporaries of Stan Laurel from the Empire's Edwardian heyday also returned to the theatre in the early '50s, although a comeback would have been impossible for the greatest name of the theatre's early days – Vesta Tilley died at eighty-three years old on 16 September 1952. A nostalgia show at the theatre in September 1951 featured Wee Georgie Wood and such music hall stalwarts as Shaun Glenville, George Robey, Hetty King, Albert Whelan, and Percy Honri, who in 1907 had presented the Empire's first Christmas show.

The veteran G.H. Elliott, who had given the Sunderland theatre such service over the years, came back in August 1953 on what was supposed to be his farewell visit, but he returned by popular demand the following September and for the last time in 1957 in the nostalgia show *Thanks for the Memory* with Hetty King, Randolph Sutton and Billy Danvers. As he had before the war he stayed with Mrs Anna Bewick who ran theatrical digs in Ashwood Street, Sunderland. During his 1954 visit he looked back over his long association with the Empire. He told the *Echo*, 'Sunderland has always been kind to me.' But he also acknowledged how fortunate he had been in that respect and how others had been less so with some entertainers being afraid to come to the town.

It was an Indian summer for family variety that was to collapse under the triple onslaught of sex, rock 'n' roll and television. Sex arrived with a vengeance in the summer of 1955. In August of that year, the French *Peep-Show* brought a frisson of mock-Gallic nudity to the theatre. It inspired much raucous behaviour from the 'louts in the gallery', complained the *Echo*'s critic. It was followed by a trickle of 'adults-only' plays: *Ladies for Hire*, about call girls, the self-

G.H. Elliott with landlady Anna Bewick in 1954.

explanatory *Call-Girl* and *The House of Shame*, which, of course, was about call girls. And then the floodgates opened for the sex-and-variety shows, most of them assembled by future porn millionaire Paul Raymond who had managed to circumvent the Lord Chamberlain's ban on nude 'action'.

As we saw during the war years, previous nude shows had featured models who had kept perfectly still; now they moved about a bit. The shows were to be a staple of the Empire programme for the next two years. There was *Montmartre Review, Nite Life USA, La Ronde Glamoresque, La Revue des Filles* and *Bubble and Peep* in which the alliterative Rhoda Rogers took a bubble bath on stage. Next up were *The French Folies Revue, Une Nuit d'Amour, Folies Striptease, The Naughtiest Girls of All* and *The Moulin Rouge Striptease Show.* As the shows became more provocative so the mock French of their titles became increasingly ridiculous. In March 1958 there came *La Grande Parade des Streep Tease*, starring Folies Frou-Frou. Strangest of them all was *Les Nues de Paris*, subtitled *Beauties and the Beast*, in which naked females shared a cage with 'forest-bred' lions. Many a formerly respectable artist hitched himself to the nude-show bandwagon. The bizarre *Girls in Cellophane* boasted naked women, primitive cling film and comedian Bill Waddington, the future Percy Sugden in *Coronation Street.*

Sunderland Echo theatre writer Philip Diack complained in his column of 17 May 1956 that such shows were 'usually deadly dull'. But he was alert to the threat they posed. He went on, ' ... the regular patrons of these shows who go to one after another in the hope of a cheap thrill can only be duped for a limited time. As for the variety-lovers, they can only be expected

Early rock 'n' rollers in Sunderland.

more often than not to stay away. It's a short-term policy then for an industry with a very small expectation of life. I believe the variety houses are doomed.'

Rock 'n' roll was to give the Empire more of a short, sharp shock. Despite the mock-Edwardian outfits of the Teddy Boys, an Edwardian theatre was not the ideal venue for the music. Rock 'n' roll did however have a profound effect on society as a whole, helping bring to an end decades of deference and it certainly dealt another heavy blow to variety. On Monday 29 October 1956 Tony Crombie and his 'Rockets' topped the bill of the Empire's first rock show. The *Echo*'s theatre critic wrote, 'Rock 'n' Roll hit Sunderland like a thunderbolt last night and the roar was so loud and frightening that many of the first-house patrons at Sunderland Empire walked out while Tony Crombie and his Rockets blared out their cacophony'. Examples of the recently invented teenager, who were no longer going to be content with performances by Issy Bonn or Dorothy Ward, were to be observed 'jiving in the aisles and screaming wildly'.

'I enjoy good jazz, and I can tap my feet to a pulsating rhythm as well as most,' declared the reviewer, 'but I found the renderings of Mr Crombie's Rockets to be nothing more than clangourous, ear-splitting uproar.'

The following week Tommy Steele made his national stage debut at the Empire. He was considered such hot stuff that a fireman had to sit on stage with him ready to put out the flames with a blanket and a bucket of sand. The Watch Committee had taken this precaution after being alarmed at rehearsal when the teenage star had connected his guitar amplifier to the mains.

Tommy Steele – Empire debutant with Sunderland fans.

The committee had another youthful act to vet a week later when skiffle star Lonnie Donegan arrived. Tommy Steele's brother Colin Hicks also headed a rock 'n' roll show at the Empire.

It was television that was to have the most profound impact on the theatre, though, diverting its entertainers and its audience. Prior to 1953 television reception on Wearside had been poor. But on Friday 1 May of that year the television mast at Pontop Pike began transmitting and life was never to be the same again in the front room or front stalls. Hundreds of television sets were delivered on Wearside; shops could barely cope with the demand. There were even television parties as 'viewers' gathered to see the new clear pictures.

For a while it seemed television and theatre could survive together as radio and theatre had in the 1930s. Some of the stars created by television came to the Empire, such as Tommy Cooper, Morecambe and Wise, Hylda Baker and Harry Worth, who had propped up many an Empire variety bill but who now came back as headliners. But ITV was launched in 1956 (the North East's ITV station Tyne Tees arrived in 1959 with Alfred and George Black Jr at the helm) and they were soon too busy in the studio and summer season to come traipsing around the country on interminable tours of the halls. As the decade drew on, the Empire, when it was not presenting nudity, generally booked those old-timers who had not been taken up by television, or staged shows in which ordinary folk pretended to be the celebrities of television and the hit parade.

In June 1958 Empire manager Jesse Challons announced that the theatre would close for a 'temporary period', the problem being a lack of top acts and a subsequent lack of audience. The Empire had a 'grand reopening' on 13 October with musicals star Edmund Hockridge and Bill

Bill Maynard on his 1958 Empire visit.

Maynard, one of the few up-and-coming entertainers it managed to secure, but it proved to be a false dawn. The theatre limped through to 2 May 1959 when it closed as a privately run venue.

Stan Laurel's old friend Trixie Wyatt had been keeping him up to date with events in Sunderland. On 22 January 1959 he had written to her from his home in Santa Monica, California. 'I can't understand why the Empire keeps open with such terrible business – that's shocking for the acts, having to play to near empty houses.' When the Empire closed, Trixie wrote to tell him. This time he replied, 'Interesting to hear that the Empire is now up for sale – am surprised this didn't happen long before now. Yes, I'm afraid Variety is a thing of the past now. The TV medium of entertainment has taken its place.' It was an assessment with which Jesse Challons would have agreed. 'We cannot make the Empire pay,' he lamented. 'The people just do not seem to want it.' However, a correspondent in the *Sunderland Echo* took issue with this. The people of Sunderland wanted a theatre, he said. What they didn't want was the 'poor choice of programme' the Empire offered.

The *Echo*'s theatre critic compared the sad occasion with the rather more dramatic demise of 'another monument of the Edwardian era, *The Titanic*'. The Empire, he wrote, went down 'with all lights blazing and the orchestra playing gay promenade music to the end.'

He continued poetically, 'And, in its way, the spectacle is just as moving; for it is hard to imagine such an old but well-found theatre, full of faded plush and gilt, suddenly transformed into a dark, empty hulk overnight.'

10

The Empire Strikes Back

Sunderland Empire was not to stay dark and empty for long. Within days of the theatre closing Sunderland Corporation was considering a rescue package. In taking over a variety hall, it was going where no local authority had gone before.

For several years the corporation had been on the look-out for a civic hall. The Victoria Hall on Toward Road had fulfilled something like that function but had been destroyed in an air raid in April 1941. Sunderland had received compensation for this from the Government and the money was now available to buy a replacement. When the Empire's neighbour, the Palace, had closed in 1956 there had been a recommendation that the council buy it at a cost of £12,000 but the scheme had been rejected. In 1959, though, when the Empire itself became available at £52,000, there was almost unanimous agreement from councillors that it should be bought.

The handful opposed to the purchase were concerned that the theatre would become a drain on the rates and the Empire was never to break even in all its years of civic control. It lost £23,830 in its first nine months. However, those in favour maintained they were not entering into a business but providing a service.

This first example of a council buying a theatre attracted national publicity. A Mr C. Murray Plumley, writing in the showbusiness weekly *The Stage*, rhapsodised, 'This paragon of civic virtues had been established not in some gentle centre of culture like Bath, Edinburgh or Stratford-on-Avon, but in a grey workaday corner of North East England.'

There was a suggestion from some correspondents however that the theatre management was providing posh shows for the 'well-to-do' at prices only they could afford. Councillor Len Harper, the Empire's greatest champion in its first two decades of civic control, hit back, 'A seat in the stalls can be obtained for less than a packet of cigarettes.' He added, 'A second-rate variety hall has been transformed into a number one theatre almost overnight.'

The old Empire as a purely commercial venture booked shows that would sell; it did not attempt to provide art for art's sake. The subsidised theatre that the Empire became after 1959 gave itself a much more difficult role; it had to strike a balance between art and commerce.

The Empire opened as Sunderland's civic theatre on Boxing Day in 1959 with Jesse Challons once again at the helm. Its first show was a panto, *Robin Hood*, with George Doonan, now sixty-two playing the Baron, and his daughter Anne as Maid Marion. The panto ran until the end of January before giving way to D'Oyly Carte Opera and then, a sign that life had not changed too much, a production of Ivor Novello's ever-popular *The Dancing Years* starring Barry Sinclair who had headed the cast of the ill-fated 1949 production.

With an injection of public money, the Empire was able to entice back some of the stars and variety was briefly reinstated. Pop star Terry Dene and comedians Chic Murray, Norman Evans and Bobby Thompson were among those heading Empire bills in the first few weeks of 1960. Gerry Dorsey, the future Engelbert Humperdinck, was second on the bill to Thompson in a June 1960 show that also included Paul Raven, the future Gary Glitter.

A brave new world – the Empire at the beginning of the 1960s.

But gradually there was a move towards drama, opera and ballet with the Empire becoming a theatre that occasionally staged variety as opposed to a variety hall that occasionally staged theatre. As the 1960s progressed, and on those weeks when the Empire was not presenting high art, the old-style variety bill began to give way to the 'one-nighters' that have been an Empire staple ever since.

The drama that began the trend was not too taxing. Michael Bentine starred in *Don't Shoot! We're English*, Bill Owen came with *Love Locked Out* and the *Carry On* films' Bernard Bresslaw headed the cast of *Master of None*. Then in 1961 there arrived the Festival Ballet (a Sunderland debut for Alicia Markova) and the Royal Philharmonic Orchestra, Sadler's Wells Opera, Ballet Rambert, Scottish National Ballet and theatre companies from Norway and the Soviet Union. In 1962 it was the turn of the Royal Ballet with Christopher Gable among its star dancers, and one of the highlights of the year was a visit by the Old Vic Company performing *Julius Caesar* and *The Tempest* with Alastair Sim as Prospero and Eileen Atkins as Miranda.

Old Vic director Joseph O'Conor officially opened the Empire restaurant on 5 October 1962 and his actors were guests at the ceremony. Councillor Harper, by now chairman of the theatre committee, told the distinguished assembly that the Empire had a record week with its Shakespeare productions. 'We're on our way,' he said. And so were coach parties from all over the North East.

In February 1963 the Empire was the venue for the first North East Theatre Festival with four weeks of productions beginning with Emrys James in the title role of *Hamlet*, followed by *Arms and the Man* with Terence Rigby and Charles West, *Twelfth Night* with Bryan Johnson as Feste, and The Royal Ballet. In the middle of the festival there was a one-night visit by the Hungarian State Orchestra.

Such fare was interspersed with lighter entertainment. Jessie Matthews starred in *Larger than Life*, Hughie Green brought his latest television hit *Double Your Money*, and Navy Lark star and future Doctor Who Jon Pertwee starred in the revue *Let's Make a Night of It*.

Above: Len Harper – the Empire's civic champion.

Opposite and left: Comedian Norman Evans and his most famous character, 'Fanny Fairbottom'.

Below: Pop star Terry Dene.

Far left: The great film actor Alastair Sim, who starred in *The Tempest*.

Left: Actor and director Joseph O'Conor in costume and character at the Empire.

Below: Television quizmaster Hughie Green on his 1963 visit to Sunderland.

Opposite, above and below: Top of the bill at last – The Beatles on their second visit to the Empire.

An imperial backdrop – Adam Faith on a subsequent visit to
Sunderland Empire.

In early 1963 teen star Helen Shapiro topped a bill that included comedian Dave Allen,
singers Danny Williams and Kenny Lynch, the Red Price Band, The Kestrels, The Honeys and a
certain up-and-coming act called The Beatles. In January 1963 The Beatles' second single *Please,
Please Me* had reached number two in the charts but even that was not enough to give them
the headlining position at the Empire a month later. On the night Saturday 9 February, there
were screaming fans in the audience but the group's performance famously failed to impress the
Echo's reviewer, the teenage Carol Roberton, who compared them unfavourably with the show's
backing band, the outfit led by Red Price. It should however be noted that at this stage in their
career, the future Fab Four were largely considered to be the chart's latest nine-day wonder;
there was no indication that they would reach the musical heights of their mature period. And
as for Mr Price's ensemble they were, as Dave Allen pointed out to me many years later, a highly
professional outfit whose instrumental prowess at that time somewhat outstripped that of Messrs
Lennon, McCartney, Harrison and Starr.

The Beatles were not to be a support act for long. Dave recalled that they were moved up the bill
as the tour progressed and their fame increased. Within a few months The Beatles were the biggest
thing in pop. They came back to the Empire as headliners on Saturday 30 November 1963 and the
theatre went Beatle crazy. In two shows the group played to more than 4,400 screaming fans.

That was quite a weekend for the Empire. On the Friday night a then little-known opera
singer called Janet Baker appeared with Bishopwearmouth Choral Society in *Elgar's Dream of
Gerontius*. It was one of her first professional engagements.

The Beatles were not the only pop stars to visit the Empire in 1963 and early 1964.
Adam Faith (who had to audition a local musician when his bassist was killed on the way to the
show), Cilla Black, Gerry and the Pacemakers (who had to be guarded by police when teenage
girls attempted to storm the stage) and Billy J. Kramer appeared there. But, by this time, the
theatre was no longer the only major music venue in the city.

11

Swinging Sunderland

The mid-1960s saw a return to a showbiz Sunderland. Dress and morals may have been entering a permissive era that would have shocked the town's Victorians but the town was almost back in the golden years of the late nineteenth century in terms of the wealth of entertainment on offer. The big difference was, however, that there was now only one professional theatre, the Empire. Show business had spilled over into the social clubs, night clubs, bingo halls and pop music venues that sprang up. There was even a Playboy Club, complete with bunny girls, down the coast in Seaham.

Billy Fury, Joe Brown and Karl Denver came to the Odeon Cinema in November 1963. Joe Brown, The Crystals, Johnny Kidd, Heinz and Manfred Mann were there the following March and in February 1964 The Rolling Stones were down the bill on a package topped by John Leyton and Mike Sarne.

Sunderland had two cabaret clubs that attracted big stars. Among those at Wetherells were Sandie Shaw, Lulu, Diana Dors, Dick Emery, Gerry and the Pacemakers, The Barron Knights, Vince Hill, Lance Percival, Kiki Dee, Lionel Blair, Kenny Ball and Peter Casson. At its rival, La Strada, the stars included Bob Monkhouse, Engelbert Humperdinck, The Shadows, Val Doonican, Joe Brown, Helen Shapiro, Chic Murray and Hylda Baker.

For its part, the Bay Hotel in Whitburn became established as an unlikely venue for big rock acts, among them Pink Floyd, Jethro Tull, Black Sabbath and Free.

Meanwhile the workmen's clubs had never had it so good. In December 1963 the Farringdon club in Sunderland opened its new concert room. It seated 575, had under-floor heating and closed-circuit television to relay shows to all other parts of the building. Bingo was one of Farringdon's attractions but clubs were now opening which offered nothing else. In October 1964 the Theatre Royal on Bedford Street reopened as a bingo hall.

A correspondent of the *Sunderland Echo*, who suggested that the Empire should be similarly converted, was no doubt voicing the views of many who were grabbed by the bingo bug at this time. Other letter writers highlighted the expense to ratepayers of maintaining the Empire as a working theatre. An *Echo* editorial in 1965 said there should be a limit to the amount of money the council was allowed to spend on the venue.

What was the Empire, which celebrated its sixtieth birthday in 1967, to do in the face of such criticism and competition? Len Harper hit back with statistics to show that attendances were rising while council subsidy was declining. Moreover he pointed out that the Empire's worth could not be reckoned merely by a glance at the balance sheet. It brought 'publicity and prestige' to the town, helped attract industry and educated the townsfolk. Like the port and shipyards it opened Sunderland to the world beyond the borough boundary.

To a large extent the Empire retreated to the higher ground. It presented Shakespeare, new drama, opera, ballet and concerts. The Royal Shakespeare Company was at the theatre in April 1965 with Ian Richardson and Michael Williams in *Comedy of Errors* as well as Ian Holm, Terence

Above: Dame Margot Fonteyn, who made guest appearances with the Royal Ballet at the Empire.

Opposite above: The Georgian State Dancers – a triumphant fortnight in Sunderland.

Opposite below (left): Sunderland actor Rod Culbertson in Swinging '60s pose.

Opposite below (right): The Empire in the mid-1960s with the Royal Ballet in residence.

Rigby and Michael Bryant in Harold Pinter's *The Homecoming*. In 1966 Prospect Theatre came with Timothy West in *The Tempest* and Julian Glover in *The Gamecock*. That year Leo McKern, Alan Dobie, James Grout and Leonard Rossiter starred in Ben Jonson's *Volpone*. In 1968 Jeremy Brett, Derek Jacobi, Ronald Pickup and John Stride brought an acclaimed all-male version of *As You Like It*, by Sir Laurence Olivier's National Theatre.

The National Youth Theatre (NYT) was a frequent visitor and many a famous name made his or her first stage appearance with NYT on tours at the Empire. A young Kenneth Cranham was in the title role of *Julius Caesar* in the autumn of 1964, future James Bond, Timothy Dalton, was Aufidius in *Coriolanus* in September 1965. Sunderland actor Rod Culbertson was Chorus in *Henry V* in September 1967. This was one of many NYT shows which featured Ed Wilson from South Shields who, a couple of decades later, became the company's director. In February 1967 former NYT star Helen Mirren, in one of her earliest professional appearances, was at the Empire in David Halliwell's award-winning *Little Malcolm and His Struggle Against the Eunuchs*. Rather more popular theatre was represented by Margaret Lockwood and Richard Todd in *An Ideal Husband*, Arthur Lowe in *Lock up Your Daughters* and Spike Milligan and Bill Kerr in Milligan's *The Bed-Sitting Room*.

Above: The Kinks – pop stars in a folk week.

Right: Virtuoso jazz pianist Oscar Peterson.

Opposite: The Bulgarian Army Song and Dance Ensemble.

Marlene Dietrich
arriving at
Newcastle airport
on her way to
Sunderland.

Also on the Empire stage were The Royal Ballet with Dame Margot Fonteyn, Sadler's Wells Opera, London Dance Theatre, Ballet Rambert, Larry Adler with the Northern Sinfonia, Basilica Opera and the Royal Philharmonic Orchestra and such greats of classical music as Yehudi Menuhin, Kurt Masur, Owen Brannigan, the viola player Phyllis Selleck, Colin Davis and Roger Norrington.

Spectacular shows from around the world were a notable success during this period. Among those who journeyed to Sunderland were the Georgian State Dance Company (which played to 22,000 people during its triumphant fortnight at the Empire), the Netherlands Dance Theatre, the Czechoslovakian State Song and Dance Ensemble, the Yugoslav National Ballet, Jose Greco and his Spanish Ballet, the African Dance Company of Guinea, the Bulgarian Army Song and Dance Ensemble and flamenco guitarist Manitas da Plata.

It was the time of the folk music boom and the Empire was caught up in it with concerts by Ewan McColl, Peggy Seeger, Tom Paxton, Cyril Tawney, Felix Doran and Martin Carthy. The Kinks even managed to crop up incongruously at the end of a folk week at the theatre.

There was also a blast of jazz at the end of the 1960s from the Oscar Peterson Quartet, Henry Red Allen, Roland Kirk, the Clarke-Boland Big Band with Johnny Griffin, Philly Joe Jones and the Modern Jazz Quartet.

Allen appeared in December 1966 as part of a package which summed up the Empire's international ambitions during this period. The great trumpeter featured in a week of concerts which also included shows by American singer-songwriter Arlo Guthrie, the rock band The Who and the most glittering and expensive star to come to Sunderland in the 1960s, the legendary Marlene Dietrich, who played to ecstatic audiences on her two nights at the theatre.

12

Alice in Sunderland

As the Empire moved into the 1970s its greatest threat came from within. A white rabbit and a little girl in a frilly frock almost killed it off in the opening months of the new decade.

In 1970 the theatre, under its ambitious director, former actor Reginald Birks, decided to produce a show of its own. The result was *You Should Have Been Here Yesterday*, 'a story of Sunderland, Wear and County', based on *Alice in Wonderland* whose author Lewis Carroll had connections with the area. It was directed and written by Gerald Frow and designed by Sean Kenny, a team with considerable West End experience. The music was written by Mike D'Abo, who was the former Manfred Mann lead singer and by then a solo artist and respected songwriter. Bill Maynard played the White Rabbit and Sally Geeson was Alice.

The show cost £30,000, most of it coming from Sunderland Council, and you could see where it went. The audience was assaulted by twenty carousel projectors, more than 900 slides, hundreds of feet of movie film and a stereo soundtrack recorded at four sessions in London. This all-encompassing entertainment had a cast of twenty actors and thirty-five musicians. The *Echo*'s critic Carol Roberton took the view, however, that *You Should Have Been Here Yesterday*, for all its technical brilliance, failed in the rather more crucial aspects of plot and performance.

The title of the show might have been a reference to the Empire's good old days of full houses and big profits. The production certainly highlighted the civic theatre's financial plight. In 1968 there had been rumours that the loss-making theatre was to be taken over by the Noble Organisation, the South Shields-based company which was running the kind of venue that the times seemed to demand: night clubs, bingo halls, cinemas and amusement arcades. But the Empire struggled on under municipal control and continued to sink deeper into the red. In 1968-69 it lost £34,817. It was a further £10,000 down the following year and £10,000 again the year after that.

In the autumn of 1970, shortly after the debacle of *You Should Have Been Here Yesterday*, Roy Todds took over as the Empire's director, Reginald Birks having announced six months earlier that he would be leaving for a theatre directorship in the south. Mr Todds declared that Mr Birks had been an artistic director but he was a practical man. Mr Todds said he would be aiming to provide a greater number of populist shows that would bring in cash rather than kudos. He boldly declared his aim 'to obliterate the subsidy, or at least cut it down to a minimum'.

Mr Birks had attempted to keep the theatre open every week of the year and provide live entertainment for most of those weeks, only resorting to films in the summer. Mr Todds, on the other hand, thriftily filled in many a gap in the programme with a movie. But he did not carry out a wholesale exercise in what we today might call 'dumbing down'. There were visits from the Royal Ballet, D'Oyly Carte, Scottish Opera, the Vienna Boys Choir and Welsh National Opera, featuring a twenty-six-year-old bearded Thomas Allen. The *Echo* described the future opera star as ' ... a talented singer from Seaham who is considered one of the most exciting discoveries of recent years'. But popular drama began to form an increasingly large part of the programme

Sally Geeson.

Reg Birks – the Empire's ambitious director.

Ken Dodd, complete with Diddy hat, out and about in Sunderland.

– Alexandra Bastedo from television's *The Champions in Conduct Unbecoming*, Ian Lavender from *Dad's Army* and Bill Maynard again in that Empire perennial *The Ghost Train*, Jack Douglas in *When The Wife's Away* and *Coronation Street's* Pat Phoenix in *Subway in the Sky*.

And there was more. That unlikely thespian Freddie 'Parrot Face' Davies starred in *Love's Luxury* and the actors from television sitcom *Never Mind the Quality Feel the Width* came in a play called *My Three Angels*. Frankie Vaughan, Kenneth McKeller, Charlie Williams, Tex Ritter, Jimmy Tarbuck and Ken Dodd appeared in one-night shows. And there were reminders of the Empire's early days with music hall productions, but they featured stars of the 1920s and later since such greats as G.H. Elliott and Gertie Gitana were no longer available (Hetty King, one of the last surviving stars of the Empire's earliest days, had been booked to return, at the age of eighty-six, in October 1969 on a *Palace of Varieties* bill but had had to pull out due to ill health). In some contrast there were two sell-out shows by the *Monty Python* team.

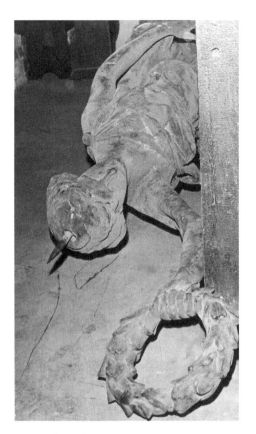

Above left: Brought out of wartime storage at last – Terpsichore.

Above right: Reopening the Empire – Victor Borge.

Despite his laudable intentions, however, Roy Todds was soon going cap in hand to the council. In 1972 the Empire was expected to lose £50,000 but Mr Todds required an extra £25,000. He was told to make do with £10,000.

Yet it was not all gloom and insolvency. In June 1972 work began on a complete overhaul of the theatre. The stalls and grand circle were re-seated, there were new entrances to the stalls and upper circle, the restaurant was decorated and the exterior floodlit. The statue of Terpsichore was taken out of storage, dusted down and put on display inside the building. And in this instance at least, the theatre was not a drain on the ratepayers. The Victoria Hall reparations fund financed the improvements just as it had paid for the Empire itself thirteen years earlier.

There were administrative changes too in the second half of 1972. The Empire Theatre Trust was set up to take over the running of the building from the council. Trust chairman Len Harper, who had steered Empire affairs since the council takeover in 1959, said the new body would speed up Empire decision making. The trust was also meant to remove the theatre from direct political control by the council, although the ruling party did supply the majority of its members.

The Empire reopened on Saturday 7 October 1972 with a concert by the great comedy musician Victor Borge.

13

'Everybody dies In Sunderland'

Many a comedian has 'died the death' at Sunderland Empire. Only one has actually died there. Sid James laughed his last dirty laugh at the Empire on Monday 26 April 1976. He was appearing in a suitably smutty comedy called *The Mating Game*. The Empire's reputation as a comedians' graveyard clung to the incident, making it seem unreal. When Empire manager Roy Todds phoned the show's producer, Bill Roberton, to break the bad news Roberton thought it was a prank.

'Sid James has just died in Sunderland,' said Todds. 'Don't worry, everybody dies in Sunderland,' replied the producer.

Back in the theatre, the Empire audience had thought it was witnessing a scripted piece of comedy, while Sid's fellow actors assumed it was comedy of the unscripted variety. Sitting next to Sid on stage was actress Olga Lowe, an old friend from his early days in his native South Africa. In 1992 she returned to the Empire to film a documentary about Sid and she told me, 'I came on, said my first lines and he answered as normal. Then I sat on the sofa with him. I said my next line and he didn't answer. His head was slumped and his eyes had gone back into his head. I thought it was a gag. Well, you would with Sid. He was such a rascal.'

Olga began to ad lib. Sid did not respond. Her ad libbing became more frantic. Realising something was seriously wrong she edged out to the wings and told the crew to bring down the curtain. Wardrobe mistress Helen Lamb ran to tell technical director Mel James, who was in his office at the back of the stage.

Mel says, 'I was the first one there, but I realised there was nothing I could do for him, so I sent for an ambulance and then went out through the tabs. It was the only time I have had to ask if there was a doctor in the house.'

Still the spirit of humour lingered. Mel's request brought a laugh from the audience. He asked again, 'In all honesty, is there a doctor in the house?'

There was indeed a doctor present, sitting in the front stalls. Usherette Irene Young met him and escorted him to the stricken actor but still it seemed ludicrous.

'The doctor came out and he thought it was a gag,' says Olga. 'But Sid was in a coma. It was awful. Ten minutes earlier, before the show, he had been the same old Sid, larking about and laughing. After the curtain came down we sat in the dressing room with a drink supplied by the theatre not knowing what to say. We were all so shocked.' Sid was taken to Sunderland Royal Infirmary. A call came about one half hour later to say he had died. He was sixty-two.

According to legend Sid has never left Sunderland Empire. There have been reports of strange goings-on in his dressing room. Les Dawson, it is claimed, refused to return to the Empire, saying he had seen a ghost while in panto in 1989. But Mel James will have none of it. 'I've never seen a ghost,' he says. 'And the only thing Les Dawson was frightened of was being caught having a cigarette by his wife.'

Above left: Sid James.

Above right: Olga Lowe – she sat next to Sid when he died.

Not only has Mel never seen a ghost at the theatre, he has never heard of anyone else seeing a ghost at the theatre – despite the claims of ghost hunters who allege that Molly Moselle, in addition to Sid James, haunts the place. But he admits there was an eerie element to the Sid James story. Partly out of respect for Sid but also for practical reasons since there was no understudy to the star, the producers decided to close the show. Mel recalls, 'We had to leave the set. It just stood there until the Thursday when we took it down. The place was like a morgue.'

For years Sunderland Empire's critics had complained it was a relic of the music hall era. In July 1974 it turned this tag to its advantage when it began to exhibit relics of the music hall era. A room above the box office was converted into Britain's National Music Hall Museum. At a cost of £30,000, it was fitted out like an Edwardian palace of varieties complete with stage, seating and a chairman's rostrum. The museum, financed by Sunderland ratepayers and the English Tourist Board, was opened by Wee Georgie Wood, one of the few survivors of the Empire's great years. Then in his seventy-eighth year, he contributed a photograph of Shaun Glenville and Dorothy Ward and programmes from four Royal Command Performances. Among the other exhibits were Ted Ray's violin, a suit worn by Stan Laurel and a cap belonging to Jimmy Clitheroe. The museum also housed thousands of playbills, comprising the most important collection of its kind in the country.

Meanwhile in the genuine Edwardian palace of varieties the entertainment was of an entirely different complexion. Status Quo played there in November 1974, Irish rock star Rory Gallagher was in concert the following month and T Rex arrived in February 1976 for a show

Right: Wee Georgie Wood meets and greets at the opening of the Music Hall Museum.

Below: Charles Hawtrey with young co-stars.

Dame Cicely Courtneidge with the Empire's portrait of Vesta Tilley.

Above left: Marc Bolan of T Rex, who had a close encounter with a Sunderland fan.

Above right: John Inman – one of the many 1970s television stars to appear at the Empire.

that was briefly interrupted by a fan who clambered on to the stage. Cliff Richard gave sell-out shows in December 1974 and November '75, as did Johnny Mathis in '77.

Coronation Street's Pat Phoenix returned in the comedy *Marriage Go-Round* with her Sunderland-born husband Alan Browning. Other television stars who stopped off at the Empire on their rounds of provinces were John Inman of *Are You Being Served?* in the comedy *My Fat Friend*, and Peter Wyngarde, who added terrifying teeth to splendid sideburns as Dracula at the Empire in April 1975. Another icon of 1970s television, the *Onedin Line's* Peter Gilmore, starred with 1960s wild child Marianne Faithful in *The Rainmaker*. There was also a return visit from one of the grand ladies of British theatre, the actress and comedienne Dame Cicely Courtneidge in the comedy *Breath of Spring* in May 1974.

Sid James was not the only star of the *Carry On* films to appear at the Empire in the mid-70s. Charles Hawtrey starred in *Snow White and the Seven Dwarfs* in the run-up to Christmas 1975. He survived the fortnight.

14

A New Stage

In 1974 Sunderland Empire moved on to a larger stage. Responsibility for funding it passed from Sunderland to the newly formed Tyne and Wear County Council. However, the county had another major theatre, Newcastle Theatre Royal, and the relationship between the two venues was not to be a happy one. For the Empire there arose a series of false dawns while the Theatre Royal moved towards a quasi-national role as the third home after Stratford and London of the Royal Shakespeare Company (RSC). In 1978 the annual residencies by the RSC began at the Newcastle theatre.

Grabbing the limelight in Sunderland were the annual cash crises. In 1977 the Empire ran up a debt of £143,000 – almost £4,000 more than was expected. It is ironic that one of the few occasions in that year that the Empire managed to cover its costs was for the final visit by the RSC. An independent report proposed the Empire should become 'the theatre of the North'. Councillor Len Harper expected stiff competition from the Theatre Royal, and he got it. Scottish Opera had enjoyed a successful three-week run at the Empire in 1978 but it was not long before it, like the RSC, was making the Theatre Royal its North East home.

In the financial year ending March 1978, the Empire's loss was £165,750. A Tyne and Wear county councillor from Sunderland called for the Empire to be closed if it could not pay its way. The following month Roy Todds, who had arrived on such a wave of optimism, said political infighting was preventing the successful running of Sunderland's theatre. He had recently announced his retirement. There was a note of weariness in his additional remarks that the Empire often came out second best to the Theatre Royal in attracting new productions to the region. Len Harper hit back, saying the formation of the Trust had taken the Empire out of party politics and that Mr Todds had a free hand in selecting shows. Councillor Harper suggested Sunderland people were more inclined to snipe at their theatre.

The Empire's fortunes took a turn for the better in the second half of 1978 when £45,000 of county council cash was spent on enlarging the theatre's orchestra pit and installing a new lighting system. It was meant to be the first stage in making the Empire the opera centre of the North East, as one of a chain of 'national' opera theatres also taking in Manchester, Liverpool and Bristol. Len Harper proclaimed the 'end of an eighteen-year fight and the beginning of a new future for the Empire'. And there was further good news with a regional production company TyneWear Theatre being set up at the Empire. However, this was at a cost. In August it was announced that the National Music Hall Museum, which had not proved to be a great attraction, was to close to make way for the theatre company's offices.

The eagerly-awaited autumn season was marred by an infamous concert by The Boomtown Rats in October 1978. Four rows of seats were pushed over, 120 were damaged at a cost of £1,500 and 'fans' spat at Bob Geldof and his band. It was the end of rock concerts at the theatre for many years.

Boomtown Rats – sparked a riot in the stalls.

There was a slight improvement in 1979 when the Empire's debt was at £137,000, which was £13,000 less than expected, and there was further talk of the theatre becoming the opera house of the North East. But the see-saw ride continued. In 1980, the debt was up to £170,000, which was £12,000 more than was expected, with productions of *The Beggars' Opera*, *Calamity Jane*, *An Ideal Husband* and *Lady Windermere's Fan* being the loss-makers. And in April of that year a report by the national theatre companies claimed the Empire was to close. The closure was denied by Empire officials but the theatre's losses continued to mount as audience figures slumped. In September the deficit was reported at almost £200,000.

Urgent talks were held to figure a way out of the problem. One radical solution was to deduct the amount overspent from the following year's county council grant to the theatre, even if this meant the door staying closed for six months of the year. Such measures were not adopted. The losses continued to mount. In 1981 the deficit was £229,264, more than £60,000 above the estimate.

In previous years the one thing that could be depended upon to pack them in was the panto. The 1978 show *Babes in the Wood*, starring Frank Ifield, had been a record-breaking success. But attendances for the 1980 panto, a particularly ill-fated affair starring Carl Wayne, formerly of the Move pop group, were almost 30,000 down on the 1979 show starring wise-cracking puppet Basil Brush.

Above: Panto record-breaker Frank Ifield.

Left: It ain't half wet mum – Windsor Davies and Melvyn Hayes.

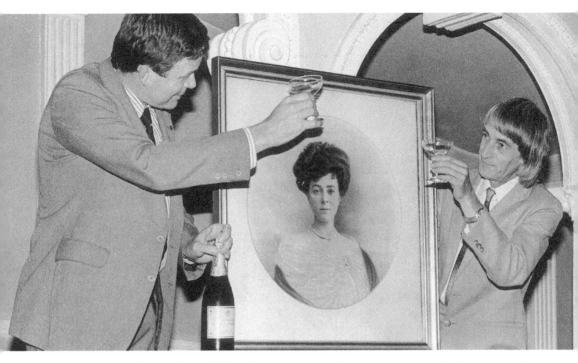

Empire managing director Russell Hills (left) and manager Ted Anker celebrate the Empire's seventy-fifth birthday.

Managing director Russell Hills brought in a series of one-night shows in 1981 with Cannon and Ball, The Shadows and Boxcar Willie among the sell-outs which helped shore up the theatre's finances. The panto that year, *Cinderella*, with *Crossroads* stars Susan Hanson and Paul Henry, was also a success, bringing in record receipts and attendances. As a result, the Empire survived to celebrate its seventy-fifth birthday in 1982, although the milestone marked the retirement of the theatre's longstanding champion, Councillor Len Harper, as chairman of its trust. And financial losses were cut by almost £70,000 to £160,362, largely thanks to *Cinderella*.

By the end of the year there was talk of the Empire becoming the national base for Gilbert And Sullivan For All, the country's only professional G&S troupe. But this dream did not materialise. By this time the Empire had also lost its resident repertory troupe with the departure for Newcastle Playhouse of Tyne Wear Theatre Company. The losses increased once more. The Empire's deficit for the financial year ending March 1982 was more than £250,000 with yet again the theatre relying on the fortunes of the panto.

Babes in the Wood at Christmas 1982 with Windsor Davies and Melvyn Hayes from television sitcom *It Ain't Half Hot Mum* did not do as well as *Cinderella*. There were further rumours of a closure. Losses were down in 1983-84 with the musical *Annie*, starring Bill Maynard, and near sell-out shows by Freddie Starr and Cannon and Ball among the successes, but were up to £282,838 in 1985, and there was talk of the Theatre Royal, as well as the Empire, being closed with the abolition of Tyne and Wear County Council in 1986. Both did stay open but the Empire was looking uncertainly to a new era in its history as it passed back into the hands of Sunderland Borough Council.

15

End of the Millennium, End of an Era

In 1991 Rudolph Nureyev might have been in the twilight of his career but his visit to Sunderland Empire that year ought still to have been a glorious moment in the history of the theatre and of its then managing director Colin Angus, who presided over the Empire during the most colourful period of its second spell under Sunderland Council control. It did result in the Empire being featured in Parliamentary debate but the mention in Hansard sprang from Wearside MP Roland Boyes feeling obliged to defend the theatre against ridicule in the national press.

Criticism of the theatre was unfair since it was Mr Nureyev, later revealed to be terminally ill, who was largely responsible for the shambles of a show that began late following last-minute changes in the programme by the temperamental star and famously featured a ballet danced in silence when a cassette player was not switched on. But it was the Empire that had to cope with outraged fans demanding their money back. It even had to fight, successfully, a legal battle with one disgruntled theatregoer who sued for the return of his ticket price and travelling expenses.

Colin Angus was a Sunderland man who had the greatest ambitions for the theatre and who succeeded in bringing many of them to fruition. He brought in big stars from America such as Dionne Warwick, Glen Campbell and Tammy Wynette. He packed them in with Billy Connolly, Michael Crawford, Van Morrison, Norman Wisdom, Ben Elton, French and Saunders, and Victoria Wood. He turned the Empire panto into the biggest in the region and one of the most star-studded in the country. He engaged a West End producer to stage the annual Christmas show and put up big sums to attract big stars. Les Dawson was snapped up in 1989 when he was the most assured panto draw in the business. Next came sitcom heart-throb Peter Howitt, later to achieve international success as a film director, and a succession of British and Australian soap stars, most notably Ken Morley, who was enticed to leave *Coronation Street* to head the 1995 Christmas cast.

Mr Angus also pushed ahead with much-needed improvements to the building itself. A new dressing room block, dance studio and bar were built at a cost of £1.1 million. The auditorium was reseated and the gallery reopened. The sound system was improved, the building was floodlit and a statue of Terpsichore was returned to the pinnacle of the theatre's tower to replace the original. And from 1985, the space formerly occupied by the music hall museum and Tyne Wear theatre company became the Empire Studio cinema, run by one of the theatre managers, Brett Childs.

But the no-win clauses kicked in. Already the largest theatre in the region, the Empire increased its capacity to just over 2,000. This was fine for Billy Connolly but smaller shows and less starry attractions had great trouble filling such a cavernous space. In Newcastle, the much smaller Theatre Royal could draw on an established audience from the entire region. The Empire had difficulty drawing from Tyneside to the north and west, and being on the coast could hardly recruit from the east.

Above left: The Empire lit up to celebrate Sunderland's new city status in 1992.

Above right: Rudolph Nureyev in his prime.

Right: Norman Wisdom in Sunderland.

Above: Glen Campbell meets fans in his Empire dressing room.

Left: Elegance personified – Empire dame Les Dawson.

Above left: Australian soap star Mark Little outside the theatre.

Above right: Ken Morley – a big leap for the Empire.

It fought yet again to achieve special status as the North East centre for ballet and opera. To this end, it won a Northern Arts grant in 1990. But the big ballet and opera companies, and the glitzy musicals for which the Empire was so ideally suited, continued to head for Newcastle. Only with the successful visits of Birmingham Royal Ballet towards the end of the 1990s did this situation begin to change.

Colin Angus built up links with the D'Oyly Carte opera company, which was revived in 1988. It was at the Empire in that year that the new company staged the glittering world premiere of its first show. Mr Angus pushed to strengthen the link by having D'Oyly Carte based in Sunderland but the plan collapsed and, adding insult to injury, the company visited Newcastle Theatre Royal instead of Sunderland Empire on its next tour.

Although the Empire had the largest stage, as well as the largest capacity in the region, that stage still wasn't big enough to accommodate the West End musicals that might have a chance of drawing a capacity crowd. In June 1997, following the sacking of Colin Angus for 'contractual irregularities' (an accusation he denied but which was upheld at an industrial tribunal), finance boss Stuart Anderson, new M.D. Symon Easton and technical director Mel James submitted a bid for £5 million from the National Lottery. Most of the money would go to enlarge the stage but funding was also sought for a new box office and stalls bar, and much-needed improvements to the toilets. There was also an ambitious proposal to stage plays and smaller shows in the old fire station next door to the theatre. Unfortunately the Arts Council, which administered National Lottery funding for the arts, had become inundated with such applications; the Empire's was one of those it had to turn down.

Left: Marion Tate, an Empire stalwart with Sadler's Wells and Birmingham Royal Ballet.

Below: Ant and Dec with Clare Buckfield in the 1998 Empire panto.

Tyneside comedian Billy Fane, an
Empire panto regular in the 1990s.

Symon Easton was, however, able to secure funding for the front-of-house improvements.
Sunderland City Council added £400,000 to £170,000 given by the Arts Council. Meanwhile
in 1995 the Empire took out a couple of loans to buy premises a few doors away on High
Street West. Administration offices were switched from the main theatre to the first floor of the
new block, and a café on the Garden Place side of the building was closed, freeing space to
accommodate a bar named in honour of Vesta Tilley. With the Arts Council and City Council
money the box office was switched to the ground floor of the High Street site. The Empire
Studio cinema was, however, closed.

Despite the improvements the Empire subsidy continued to rise. In 1999, following the
departure of Mr Easton, the local authority received an offer from Apollo Leisure to take over
the running of the building and, faced with that ever-increasing deficit (by the turn of the
millennium it stood at £775,000), it decided to put the Empire under private management for
the first time in forty years. The contract went out to tender and Apollo was awarded a twelve-
year contract, starting on 1 October 2000. Through its American links and the group purchasing
power of its British network of twenty-six theatres, the company promised to bring in the
highest quality musicals and one-nighters. It also aimed to drastically reduce the council subsidy.
It began by making Empire history by appointing the theatre's first female managing director,
Sunderland-born Debbie Garrick.

16

New Millennium, New Beginning

The change in Sunderland Empire's fortunes over the last seven years has been as unexpected as it has been welcome. The switch to private management was not universally applauded. Sceptics suggested the company would milk the theatre for a few years and then depart, leaving the Empire in a worse state. Even those who were broadly in favour barely dared hope for success. There had been, as we have seen, several false dawns.

The first big show following the takeover provided ammunition for the sceptics, even though it had been assembled by the previous management's pantomime producers. The *Sleeping Beauty* of Christmas 2000, starring *EastEnders* actor Craig Fairbrass, was not a hit. Within days of the new regime beginning its reign it was announced that the Empire had required £310,000 more than expected to keep it open during 2000 – taking the annual council subsidy up to a record £950,000.

Events in America were to have a major influence on the theatre's fortunes. Although Apollo Leisure won the contract to run the Empire, it had by 1 October 2000 been taken over. It had initially been acquired by American entertainment group SFX, the world's largest combined production, promotion and management company. It owned 116 venues in the States, and produced and promoted touring Broadway shows, concerts and sporting events. A few months later SFX was in turn taken over by Clear Channel, America's largest radio group. For the first time since the 1950s Sunderland Empire was not on its own; it was part of a worldwide entertainment organisation.

Big shows began to arrive, beginning with *Saturday Night Fever*, which had its regional premiere at the Empire, as did *Chicago* in December 2001 and the Lloyd Webber musical *Whistle Down the Wind* in February 2002. *Peter Pan*, the 2001 Christmas show, was a huge success with Brian Blessed as a splendidly larger-than-life Captain Hook. The show broke box-office records.

By the time the 2001-02 accounts were published, the Empire subsidy was still, at £783,068, beyond 1999's critical level of £750,000, but it was down on the previous year's high, and continued to drop. In 2002-03 it was £609,841; in 2003-04 it was £517,754; in 2004-05 it was £491,171; and in 2005-06 it was £476,756. The uncertainty had been removed from the city council's budgeting for the theatre. Each year Sunderland City Council now paid a management fee and a contribution to the maintenance of the Empire. The risk and potential profits were Clear Channel's but if the company made a profit the council received a share. It was a win-win arrangement.

In April 2002 a stalls bar was opened in place of the old box office, with improved wheelchair access to the theatre. Then, in the autumn of that year, a lavish restaging of *The King and I* proved a landmark production for the Empire. It had punters flocking to it from as far away as South Yorkshire and the Scottish borders. Two weeks into its three-week run it became the most profitable in Empire history. Such shows not only made local people believe once again in their theatre, their success encouraged other producers to bring their shows to Sunderland.

Right: Brian Blessed – a larger-than-life presence as Captain Hook.

Below: Shades of Tom Mix, equine star of the colourful Chisinau State Opera.

Birmingham Royal Ballet persisted with its laudable policy of bringing dance of the highest quality for the lowest possible ticket price and after brief relationships with Opera North, Scottish Opera and the revived Carl Rosa, the Empire struck up a lasting friendship with the Opera And Ballet International company of the irrepressible Ellen Kent, who staged traditional productions of popular opera with singers from Eastern Europe (chiefly Moldova) and added attractions, ranging from dancing stallions and birds of prey to naked sopranos and tanks of koi carp.

It took more than even these crowd-pleasers, however, to ensure the future of the theatre. As part of the takeover deal the new management company had been required to prepare a plan for the large-scale redevelopment of the Empire. A report submitted to Sunderland City Council in 2003 stated that the long-planned improvements to the theatre, notably the enlargement of the stage, were now urgently needed.

The Empire was about to get lucky. When carrying out their survey of the Empire the people at Clear Channel figured they could enlarge the performing area without demolishing the whole of the back stage. All of a sudden the improvements became rather more affordable.

Further good fortune followed. Sunderland City Council had just had a windfall from the sale of its council houses and its shares in Newcastle Airport. As a result £4.6 million was stumped up to carry out the Empire work, the bulk of it coming from the city (£1.5 million), Clear Channel (£1.1 million) and regional development body One NorthEast (£1.5 million). Since the theatre was going to be closed for a while the opportunity was taken to carry out other much-needed improvements and One NorthEast was able to obtain further cash to renovate the Empire auditorium for the first time since the mid-1980s.

Shortly before the builders moved in their plans had to be rapidly revised. The Empire was told it could have *Starlight Express* for Christmas 2004/05 if the stage and auditorium work could be completed by the beginning of December (work on a new dressing room block was given until the following spring). It was an offer that could not be refused. The scaffolding went up in April 2004 and work proceeded smoothly, if rather frantically, until the summer when the rains came and everything ground to a halt. After an extremely frantic autumn the Empire obtained its licence to reopen at 6.15 p.m. on 8 December. The curtain rose on the first performance of Starlight Express at 7.30 p.m. on 8 December.

During the nine-month closure, the longest period the Empire had ever been without shows, the theatre's old fly tower above the stage was partially demolished and a new one, a third higher, was built to accommodate not only bigger and heavier backdrops and pieces of scenery, but also a greater number which could be 'flown up' when not in use. Within that tower two galleries were installed, as was a new counterweight system and twenty-five new 'flying' lines, taking the total up to fifty-nine.

The Empire's grand proscenium arch was left intact but the space behind it was extended – two staircases, an office and a toilet were removed – so that the stage no longer tapered towards the back. In addition, the stage's rake, or slope, was removed. Beneath the stage the orchestra pit was deepened and the entire stage area was rewired. The auditorium was redecorated, the stalls re-carpeted, seats were replaced or repaired in the stalls and dress circle, and a new fire alarm and evacuation system installed. Behind the stage an enlarged, canopied scene dock could now accommodate the pantechnicons delivering large props and scenery for those largest West End shows. The lorries could even, if necessary, be driven on to the back of the stage.

The official first night of *Starlight Express* on 9 December 2004 had echoes of the Empire's first opening night in 1907. As then, the audience was packed with local and London bigwigs, as the creative team behind the Clear Channel production and executives from the company's head office sat alongside the leading players of Sunderland civic and commercial life.

Above: The Empire's new fly tower rises over the old dressing room block.

Right: The crowds turn out for Miss Saigon.

Technicians prepare the stage for *Starlight*.

Spectacular start to a new era – *Starlight Express* performers. (Photograph by Alessandro Pinna).

The car's the star – *Chitty Chitty Bang Bang*. (Photograph © Tristran Kenton).

Left: Amy Nuttall as Eliza Doolittle in Cameron Mackintosh and the National Theatre's production of Lerner and Loewe's *My Fair Lady*. (Photograph by Michael Le Poer Trench © Cameron Mackintosh Limited)

Below: The Count and Countess of Wessex on the Empire stage.

Just like then, the performance had to do more than merely entertain – it had to set the scene for a whole new theatrical era.

Much to the distinguished audience's relief, the evening passed off without mishap. Watching from the wings, Empire managing director Dominic Stokes, who had replaced Debbie Garrick in 2002, wiped his brow and let out an enormous sigh of relief as *Starlight* was granted its well-deserved standing ovation.

There quickly followed a second West End show which the Empire could not have accommodated before its refit. *Miss Saigon* opened at the end of January 2005 and was, if anything, a greater triumph, running most of the way until Easter and breaking *Starlight's* box office record. At the *Starlight Express* opening night David Ian, managing director of Clear Channel Europe, had stepped on to the stage to announce that a third West End hit, *Chitty Chitty Bang Bang*, would have its UK provincial premiere at the Empire in December 2005. Here was proof of the theatre's new status within the business. With its £1 million car, the world's most expensive prop, it arrived to beat the box office records of its illustrious predecessors. A major revival of *My Fair Lady* and big-name productions of *Chicago* and *Scrooge* were among the West End shows that followed.

In the build-up to its centenary, the revived Empire, by now managed by Paul Ryan, was officially reopened by the Earl and Countess of Wessex.

If they're looking down from that dress circle in the sky, the founders of Sunderland Empire will not be surprised to see their theatre reaching its 100th birthday but they will surely be astonished to see the significance it has acquired for Sunderland. When Richard Thornton died in 1922, Sunderland still had a handful of grand theatres. A decade later the Empire was more or less on its own as a venue for regular, first-class live entertainment – and so it has stayed, apart from a few years when it had competition from cabaret and social clubs. By the end of the century it didn't even have competition from cinemas. Today it has a multiplex a few blocks away with, ironically enough, the same name, but the Empire cinema, splendid though it is, is not quite in the same league as its namesake theatre. Because it has been for most of its life Sunderland's only professional theatre, the Empire has occupied a prominent place in the consciousness of Sunderland people. Along with the football club it is – now that the shipyards, collieries and Vaux Brewery have closed – one of the few things for which Sunderland is famous.

Not only is Sunderland Empire still here 100 years later, it is in better health than it has been since the days of Dick Thornton – that is something that would certainly surprise most of Thornton's successors. As we have seen, Sunderland Empire has not had it easy. It has had a century of adapting to changes in entertainment tastes and technology. It has weathered economic slump and bureaucratic upheaval. It has returned from the dead, beaten off calls for its closure and clung on despite running up huge losses. It has survived the arrival of cinema, radio, the recording industry and television, and the death of variety. It has even survived the digital revolution. It has done so because it has become such a symbol of Sunderlandness but also because there is no substitute for live entertainment, particularly when it is staged in such a great, historic building as the Empire – and that's as true today in the age of *Starlight Express* and *Miss Saigon* as it was in the heyday of G.H. Elliott, Wee Georgie Wood and Gertie Gitana. It will also be true in another 100 year's time.

Bibliography

Anderson, Albert, *A Century of Sunderland Cinemas*, Black Cat Publications, 1996

Bailey, Peter (ed), *Music Hall: The Business of Pleasure*, Open University Press, 1986

Bratton, J.S. (ed), *Music Hall: Performance and Style*, Open University Press, 1986

Busby, Roy, *British Music Hall, An Illustrated Who's Who from 1850 to the Present Day*, Elek, 1976

Chaplin, Charles, *My Autobiography*, Bodley Head, 1964

Corfe, Tom, *A History of Sunderland*, Frank Graham, 1973

Corfe, Tom (ed), *The Buildings of Sunderland 1814-1914*, Tyne and Wear County Council Museums, 1983

De Frece, Lady, *Recollections of Vesta Tilley*, Hutchinson, 1934

Disher W.W., *Winkles and Champagne*, 1984

Dodds, G.L., *History of Sunderland*, Albion Press, 1995

Evans, Len and Bullar, Gary R., *'The Performer' Who's Who in Variety*, The Performer Ltd, 1950

Foster, Andy and Furst, Steve, *Radio Comedy 1938-1968*, Virgin, 1996

Fountain, Nigel, *Lost Empires: The Phenomenon of Theatres Past, Present and Future,* Cassell 2005

Gallagher, J.P., *Fred Karno, Master of Mirth and Tears*, 1971

Gammond, Peter, compiled by, *Your Own, Your Very Own! A Music Hall Scrapbook*, Ian Allan, 1971

Green, Benny, *The Last Empire, A Music Hall Companion*, Pavilion, 1986

Hawkins, Desmond, *When I Was*, Macmillan, 1989

Hudd, Roy, *A Book of Music Hall, Variety and Showbiz Anecdotes*, Robson, 1993

Hudd, Roy with Hindin, Philip, *Roy Hudd's Cavalcade of Variety Acts, A Who Was Who of Light Entertainment 1945-1960*, Robson Books, 1997

Jenkins, Alan, *The Forties*, Heinemann, 1977

Kilgarriff, Michael, *Grace, Beauty and Banjos*, Oberon Books, 1998

McCabe, John, *Charlie Chaplin*, Robson Books, 1992

McCarthy, Albert, *The Dance Band Era*, Spring Books, 1971

Marriot, A.J., *Chaplin Stage by Stage*, Marriot Publishing, 2005

Marriot, A.J., *Laurel and Hardy, The British Tours*, published by the author, 1993

Mellor, G.J., *They Made Us Laugh*, Kelsall, 1982

Mellor, G.J., *The Northern Music Hall*, Frank Graham, 1970

Milburn, G.E. and Miller, S.T. (eds), *Sunderland: River, Town and People*, Thomas Reed Printers Ltd, 1988

Mitchenson, Joe and Mander, Raymond, *British Music Hall*, Gentry Books, 1974

Newton, H. Chance, *Idols of the Halls*, 1928, republished by EP Publishing Ltd and British Book Centre Inc, 1975

Priestley, J.B., *Lost Empires*, Everyman, 1965

Robinson, Alistair, *Sunderland – A City for a New Future*, City of Sunderland, 2006.

Robinson, David, *Chaplin, His Life and Art*, Collins, 1985

Rust, Brian, *British Music Hall on Record*, Gramophone, 1979

Sell, Michael and Earl, John, *The Theatres Trust Guide to British Theatres, 1750-1950*, A&C Black, 2000

Wilmut, Roger, *Kindly Leave the Stage! The Story of Variety, 1919-1960*, Methuen, 1985

Wood, Georgie, *I Had To Be Wee*, Hutchinson, 1948